Baseball's
Great Dynasties
THE
Dodgers

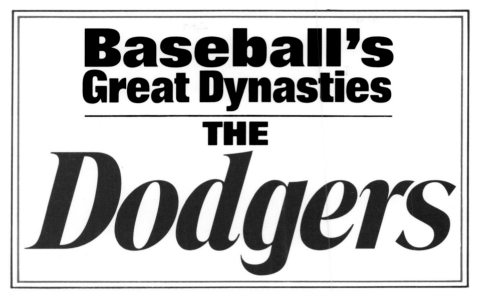

Baseball's Great Dynasties
THE
Dodgers

Peter C. Bjarkman

GALLERY BOOKS
An imprint of W.H. Smith Publishers Inc.
112 Madison Avenue
New York, New York 10016

For Carl Erskine, a fan's delight, then and now . . .

Published by Gallery Books
A Division of W H Smith Publishers Inc.
112 Madison Avenue
New York, New York 10016

Produced by
Brompton Books Corp.
15 Sherwood Place
Greenwich, CT 06830

ISBN 0-8317-0655-4

Printed in Hong Kong

10 9 8 7 6 5 4 3 2 1

PICTURE CREDITS

The Bettmann Archive: 11, 13.
Malcolm Emmons: 2, 6(left), 58(left), 61, 62(bottom), 63,
   64(both), 65, 66, 68(left), 69, 70(right).
Nancy Hogue: 7(top right, bottom left), 68(right),
   71(left), 72.
National Baseball Library, Cooperstown, NY: 10, 15, 17,
   21, 22, 23(both), 36, 38(top), 42, 67.
Ponzini Photography: 6(right), 7(top left, bottom right),
   60, 70(left), 71(right), 74(top), 75(bottom), 76(both),
   77.
UPI/Bettmann Newsphotos: 1, 3, 4-5, 8, 9, 12, 14,
   16(both), 18, 19, 20, 24, 25, 26, 27, 28, 29(both),
   30(both), 31, 32, 33, 34, 35, 37, 38(bottom), 39, 40, 41,
   43, 44, 45, 46(both), 47, 48, 49, 50, 51, 52, 53(both), 54,
   55, 56, 57, 58-59, 62(top), 73(both), 74(bottom),
   75(top).

ACKNOWLEDGEMENTS

The author and publisher would like to thank the following people who have helped in the preparation of this
book: Barbara Thrasher, who edited it; Don Longabucco,
who designed it; Rita Longabucco, who did the picture
research; and Cynthia Klein, who prepared the index.

Page 1: *Gil Hodges slides safely home in 1949 game action against the Pittsburgh Pirates. Dodger Bruce Edwards ducks as he sees the throw come in high.*

Page 2: *Sandy Koufax displays the Hall-of-Fame style that earned back-to-back Cy Young Awards in 1965 and 1966.*

Page 3: *The 1955 World Champion Brooklyn Dodgers pose in Ebbets Field; this was to be the only World Series winner in 68 full years of Brooklyn National League play.*

Below: *Tom Lasorda and his players rush from the dugout to celebrate the 1981 World Championship victory over the New York Yankees.*

Contents

Preface

First came the notorious Daffiness Dodgers of the 1920s and 1930s, apparent big-league pretenders bungling into reckless traffic jams along the basepaths. This was a team cursed with notoriety as Brooklyn's favorite hopeless Bums, and saddled with seemingly endless rosters of colorful but hapless baseball clowns. The Dodgers' Babe Herman was himself only a small step behind that other famous New Yorker known as Babe, both in civilian exploits and in hitting prowess (Herman hit .393 in 1930). Then there was baseball's premier clown prince, Casey Stengel, who disguised fourteen seasons of often-brilliant outfield play in five big-league cities with unparalleled onfield antics, at the same time fashioning baseball's most memorable brand of personal folk lingo. Wilbert Robinson managed two full decades in Brooklyn with little championship success, yet also built a legacy of Ebbets Field high jinks and shenanigans

unmatched in all baseball history. Pennants and World Championships were lost on such ballpark aberrations as Wambsganss' unprecedented World Series unassisted triple play, Mickey Owen's decisive dropped third strike, Herman legging a sure two-bagger into baseball's most infamous double play, and numerous such episodes of unforgivable baseball misadventure. Ebbets Field from its earliest years, in fact, became sanctified in baseball lore as a site where unlikely high jinks always seemed to outstrip routine diamond play. And yet the Brooklyn diehard faithful remained, throughout it all, the most loyal in the annals of baseball fandom.

Later arose the glorious "Boys of Summer" Dodgers, immortalized for all ages by the prose of Roger Kahn – a matchless baseball dynasty artfully constructed in the early 1940s by the innovative Larry MacPhail (founder of big-league night baseball) and Branch Rickey (architect of baseball's

Below left: *Don Drysdale pitched in the shadow of Sandy Koufax, yet the 60s also belonged to this crafty righty.*

Below right: *Mike Scioscia became the regular Dodger catcher after 1981.*

Opposite top left: *Fernando Valenzuela, 1981 Cy Young winner.*

Opposite top right: *Reggie Smith hit over .300 in 1977 and 1980.*

Opposite bottom left: *Ron Cey remains the Los Angeles Dodgers' career HR leader.*

Opposite bottom right: *Eddie Murray brought 333 career homers when he arrived from Baltimore in 1989.*

Above: *Key players who led the Brooklyn Dodgers to a 4-2 victory over the Yankees during the first game of the 1952 World Series celebrate in the Ebbets Field dressing room. Left to right: winning pitcher Joe Black; Duke Snider, who hit a decisive two-run homer; Mgr. Chuck Dressen; Pee Wee Reese, who also homered; and Jackie Robinson, who homered for Brooklyn as well. The Dodgers would eventually lose the Series in a heartbreaking seventh game, their third of five October losses to the hated Yankees during the glorious "Boys of Summer" decade.*

first farm system), and nominated by baseball historians like John Bowman and Joel Zoss as perhaps the greatest National League team of all time. In one ten-year period, from 1947 through 1956, the Dodgers of Brooklyn won six pennants and finished a tight second three times. Had three within-reach pennants not been squandered in the final playing days of 1946, 1950 and 1951, the final tally might well have been an unprecedented nine flags in an 11-year span; only 19 more victories over that stretch would have meant an unimaginable 11 consecutive National League crowns.

More recent seasons have witnessed the efficient and businesslike Los Angeles ball club of the much maligned Walter F. O'Malley and his family heirs – transplanted West Coast Dodgers boasting a wholesome, new image and asserting relentless domination over National League baseball across the past three decades. It is one of modern baseball's least publicized facts that but two field bosses have guided Dodger fortunes since that first Brooklyn World Championship year of 1955. In the 30-odd seasons following the team's arrival in California, Walter Alston and his loyal protégé Tommy Lasorda have claimed for the City of Angels five World Titles and nine National League flags, plus eight

additional Western Division crowns since the inauguration of divisional play in 1969. Few franchises have ever enjoyed such a relentless string of baseball victories. Nor have any approached the appeal of O'Malley's Dodgers at the turnstile – seven seasons of over three million paying customers drawn into Chavez Ravine, plus the top six all-time single-season attendance figures as well. And while many ball clubs have seen fit to commandeer the hollow title of America's Team, no franchise in baseball history has so persistently captured the imaginations and the rabid following of so many fans.

Few professional baseball clubs have displayed such distinctive personalities throughout their history as have the Dodgers of Brooklyn and Los Angeles. The present-day Los Angeles ball club of Walter F. O'Malley and his immediate successors provides an idealized portrait of today's impersonally efficient pro sports franchise. Unchallenged at the box office as baseball's premier drawing card, the Dodgers are a consistent National League powerhouse that has brought five World Championships, nine league pennants, and seven divisional titles to the City of Angels during three storied decades of West Coast major-league play. For skeptical baseball fans around the nation, the O'Malley-

Alston-Lasorda Dodgers of the past decade suggest the very epitome of the streamlined winning baseball organization, and of the professional on-field conduct expected of today's high-salaried ballplayers.

This is a far different public image from the one paraded before the baseball world by the Daffy Dodgers of the 1920s and 1930s under such colorful field managers as Wilbert Robinson and Casey Stengel, or the lovable yet exasperating 1940s Brooklyn Bums inspired by the controversial Leo Durocher and the daring Jackie Robinson. Even the glorious "Boys of Summer" Dodgers – masters of the National League throughout the early and mid-1950s – remain one of baseball's most memorable teams, famed for daring and pugnacious play and for the fanaticism of their Ebbets Field faithful. While the Dodgers of O'Malley have become entrenched in the popular imagination of most baseball fans across the country as complacently efficient winners, the earlier stumblebums of Brooklyn have withstood the decades as storied progenitors of baseball's most famous plaintive loser's lament – "Wait until next year!"

One need only to compare the quaint baseball setting of Brooklyn's Ebbets Field with the sprawling suburban neatness of Los Angeles Dodger Stadium. Now predated by ancient Wrigley Field alone among existing National League ball parks, Dodger Stadium today stands as perhaps baseball's unrivaled aesthetic playing facility – the crown jewel of the Dodgers' polished West Coast professional image. O'Malley's great pleasure-palace at Chavez Ravine – with its 56,000 seats on five different grandstand levels and its parking facilities for 16,000 cars on 21 terraced lots – is also, however, the ultimate reflection of the rootless, faceless, surburban image associated with Southern California baseball.

The story of the Dodgers is largely the dramatic saga of this evolution from one of baseball's most lamentable if beloved ball clubs to one of its most potent dynasties during the decades under Larry MacPhail, Branch Rickey and Walter O'Malley. It is also the story of two of professional baseball's most daring front office experiments – Branch Rickey's bold challenge to baseball's loathsome color barriers at the close of World War II, and Walter O'Malley's subsequent break with baseball's rigid geographical boundaries a brief decade later. Rickey opened up the game to a new generation of talented black and Hispanic athletes who provide the lifeblood of today's professional game; by accelerating baseball's coast-to-coast expansion, O'Malley brought eyewitness baseball fandom into

markets from Houston to Anaheim to Seattle and provided hometown teams for millions of fans who had known nothing but a lifetime of radio baseball.

Above all else, however, Dodger history recounts the exciting exploits of some of baseball's greatest superstars – the incomparably graceful slugger of the 1950s, Duke Snider; the dashing, dark-skinned pioneer who carried the hopes and aspirations of his entire race, Jackie Robinson; those silent stalwarts of Brooklyn's greatest teams during the final New York decade, Roy Campanella and Gil Hodges; Sandy Koufax, the mid-1960s' most dominant fastballer and perhaps the most electrifying southpaw in baseball's entire glamorous history; the incomparable 1920s' pitching tandem of Dazzy Vance and Burleigh Grimes, together striking certain fear into the hearts of a generation of National League hitters; the charismatic, Mexican left-hander, Fernando Valenzuela, capturing the early 1980s by storm and single-handedly restoring flamboyance and respectability to the once-proud Dodgers franchise.

From the loveable Daffy Bums of Flatbush to the laid-back California Golden Boys of the 1980s, decades of Dodger teams emerge from the chapters that follow. This volume brings to life the lost legends, the zany and often unforgettable moments, the storied individual performances highlighting well over a century of Dodgers baseball – from Brooklyn to Los Angeles. The most sizzling pennant races are nostalgically recounted here, while the heart-wrenching, final-day pennant defeats are also dramatically retold. Readers are invited to pass once again through a century of National League baseball fact and folklore, and to discover in these pages the inside story of one of America's all-time favorite baseball teams.

Above: *With little over six weeks remaining until opening day on April 10, 1982, this rare aerial view shows nearly complete Dodger Stadium in Chavez Ravine and its proximity to the Los Angeles Civic Center. When mud from recent rains dried sufficiently, sod was laid for the playing field and bleachers constructed across the open end of the stadium (foreground). Only painting and erection of the famous prefabricated partitions in the interior of the ballpark then remained. Somehow the work was completed on schedule, and a crowd of 52,564 settled into the spanking new Taj O'Malley to see the Dodgers lose 6-3 to the Cincinnati Reds in the inaugural of the West Coast's new baseball pleasure palace.*

1. Those Daffy Brooklyn Dodgers of Not So Long Ago

Below: *A proud Mrs. Ed McKeever, wife of the vice-president of the Brooklyn Baseball Club, raises a new flag for the first game at Ebbets Field on April 9, 1913. The first Ebbets Field game was a 1-0 loss to the Philadelphia Phillies, with 12,000 in attendance for the historic game. From the day of its birth there was no doubt that Ebbets Field would be the scene for some of baseball's daffiest moments, as this very flag-raising was delayed when aids forgot to bring the all-important flag.*

O'Malley brought the Dodgers of the 1960s and 1970s more than just a transformation of personality. In five decades of play in Brooklyn, between their inaugural season in the National League and the arrival of Hurricane Larry Mac-Phail as General Manager and Leo Durocher as field boss at the end of the 1930s, Brooklyn's professional baseball team was a laughingstock around the league and something less than a proud diversion for Brooklyn's faithful fans at home. Not that Brooklynites didn't love their team; yet the Ebbets Field faithful usually had little enough to cheer about and less still to celebrate.

The first full 50 seasons of Brooklyn National League baseball witnessed a sparse four pennants and not a single World Championship year. Thirty-six seasons – a full two-thirds of those played in Brooklyn before the second World War – saw the Dodgers finish in fifth place or lower. There was always plenty of raw entertainment at the ballpark in Flatbush,

of course – such colorful characters as Babe Herman, Casey Stengel, Hack Wilson and Dazzy Vance donned Brooklyn uniforms in those days and supplied at least unmatched buffoonery where solid baseball fundamentals were almost always woefully lacking. These were the decades of the Daffiness Dodgers teams which supplied Brooklyn baseball forever with its indelible losers image.

Even the glorious teams of the 1940s and 1950s – managed by Shotton, Dressen and Alston, and starring such Cooperstown immortals as Jackie Robinson, Roy Campanella, Duke Snider, and Pee Wee Reese – were unable to totally escape the "loveable losers" image which plagued Brooklyn ball clubs right down to their final seasons in Ebbets Field. While dominating the National League during the decade from the end of World War II until the dawn of baseball's western expansion, these Dodgers seemed to always be fodder for the cannons of those unbeatable Yankees when baseball's October Classic rolled around.

This may well have been one of baseball's most talented teams during that golden epoch of the 1950s, but it was also only the second best team in the City of New York!

Through seven decades of residence in the sprawling borough of Brooklyn, the Flatbush Dodgers were anything but the proficient and businesslike tinsel-town ball club that later methodically conquered all upstart National League rivals from its new West Coast home. The Dodgers of an earlier era were relentlessly dogged by a far different set of ballpark images – those of madcap clowns and buffoons in baggy baseball flannels, catastrophic traffic jams cluttering the basepaths, insanely zealous fans rooting vainly for chronic losers. Perhaps in no age of baseball history has a team been more passionately beloved and revered by the locals, more intensely followed, more intimately taken to heart as the very spirit and soul of the community that housed them. Such was the fate of Dodgers teams calling Brooklyn home from the earliest National League years to the middle of the present century. Yet no team was also more reviled for their failures and blunders than these same Dodgers, and perhaps only the "Gas House Gang" Cardinals of the 1930s provided as many excuses for unbridled derision or more legitimate disheartening blows to the local baseball faithful.

The name "Dodgers" is itself almost synonymous with strange and often unique baseball incidents from past decades. Historians now claim for Brooklyn the first enclosed bleachered ballpark, and transplanted Englishman Henry Chadwick fashioned baseball's first box score and initial rule book while reporting local games for the fledgling *Brooklyn Eagle*. Ebbets Field itself was constructed upon a steamy garbage heap in the notorious Pigtown section of Flatbush, and no ballpark in baseball history was actually more quickly obsolete or sooner in need of drastic refurbishing. Charles Ebbets, it turns out, was adding extensive grandstand sections to his proud park within a mere seven seasons of its original opening. Yet on the afternoon of its birth, April 9, 1913, Ebbets Field was appropriately baptized as the original home of true baseball daffiness. Thousands of fans lined up outside the palatial brick structure in hope of opening day seats, only to wait well beyond scheduled game time for the park gates to open. It seems the harried park superintendent had misplaced the front gate key. That first historic ball game at Ebbets Field was also covered by hordes of angered sportswriters forced to work from their cramped seats within the grandstand, since the builder had also bungled his opening day assign-

ment – somehow neglecting to install the required ballpark press box.

Even from its maiden season of 1913, cramped and creaky Ebbets Field seemed pre-destined to provide an unmatched setting for eccentric baseball characters, inept and often exasperating home team play, continuous front-office wrangling (usually accompanied by near insolvency in the team's coffers), plus some of the most bizarre on-field events of baseball's rich history. While other proud New York franchises – the heroic Yankees of the Bronx and the hated Giants of Harlem – offered endless supplies of true baseball heroes, storybook pennant campaigns, and countless memorable diamond achievements, the Bums of Flatbush spawned insufferably long dry spells of second-division baseball fortunes. But in the process they sowed the seeds, as well, for one of baseball's most enduring literary legends.

Numerous landmark incidents today attest to the unprecedented follies of early Brooklyn professional baseball. The baneful curveball – scourge of hitters throughout the ages – was one among many baseball innovations first introduced by often otherwise undistinguished Brooklyn stalwarts. In this case the obscure author was an unsung nineteenth-century hurler named William "Candy" Cummings from Brooklyn's early amateur baseball days. A most unconventional nineteenth-century baseball deal also once transplanted nearly the entire Baltimore Orioles championship lineup of the late 1890s to Brooklyn, lock, stock, and barrel, and thus purchased for the Dodgers two early and perhaps somewhat tainted league pennants. This 1899 event, orchestrated by the crafty Charles Ebbets, remains baseball's most unconventional franchise shift, and one nearly inex-

Above: *An aerial view of picturesque Ebbets Field in the 1940s. This was the home of one of baseball's most beloved teams, the history-making "Boys of Summer," streaking through 10 National League campaigns, from Jackie Robinson's debut in 1947 to his premature retirement in 1957. This team may well have finished only second best in New York, season after season. Yet today the Dodgers of Reese, Campanella, Snider and Hodges remain foremost in the hearts of nostalgic Brooklyn fans. Ebbets Field was perhaps the very epitome of intimate and accessible baseball environments.*

Famed Manager Casey Stengel bangs out fungoes in 1934 Dodgers Spring Training camp at Orlando, Florida. A fireplug outfielder for Brooklyn teams of two decades earlier, Stengel's three seasons as Brooklyn manager proved less than successful, never providing higher than a weak, fifth-place finish. Stengel would later return to haunt his former club as manager of the awesome Yankee teams which would sweep the World Series with regularity from the Dodgers of the 1950s. Casey was also one of the game's great original showmen.

plicable from today's modern business framework, where such conspiratorial deals would be promptly voided by the game's governing bodies.

The game's first ill-fated experiment with electronic public address systems, now such standard fare in the modern-day stadium, also transpired during Charlie Ebbets' colorful Brooklyn years. Having replaced Ebbets Field barkers toting hand-held megaphones with an ingenious metal plate affixed to the ground near home plate, Ebbets experienced near disaster when the new contraption suddenly filled the air with the cursing of Brooklyn stalwart Ivan Olsen, who raged profanely at an umpire's unwelcomed decision. Ebbets personally led a team of groundskeepers armed with fire axes on to the field to destroy the offending equipment, thus temporarily suspending his ill-founded experiment in stadium electronics.

From the outset, daffiness was the proper byword of Dodgers baseball, and Brooklyn fans – themselves consistently the rowdiest and most colorful in the land – could always count on lively ballpark entertainment, if not sustained baseball success. Baseball's quickest recorded ejection reputedly happened in Ebbets Field, when Dodgers star catcher Al Lopez made an unscheduled visit to the showers only moments after the game's opening pitch. Bizarre and much ballyhooed off-field incidents were commonplace as well, headlined by manager

Wilbert Robinson's aborted stunt of catching a baseball dropped from a hovering biplane during spring training revelries of 1912. Madcap exploits by baseball's unique clown prince, Charles Dillon "Casey" Stengel – Brooklyn outfielder of the pre-World-War-I era and then manager for a short stint in the mid-1930s – climaxed with Casey's unique hidden bird trick, enacted before a stunned and unappreciative umpire at Ebbets Field's home plate. Stengel (with the Pirates at the time) doffed his cap in the batter's box and a captured sparrow fluttered from his head only seconds before the enraged arbiter sent Stengel winging on his own journey to the showers. Such outrageous on-field shenanigans were numerous in Brooklyn, but none surpassed an infamous 1926 Sunday afternoon incident featuring the immortal Babe Herman, a unique baseball moment which found "Brooklyn's Babe" and two additional Dodger teammates all hugging third base at the same embarrassing moment.

The origin of professional baseball in the borough of Brooklyn predates the National League Dodgers by little more than a full decade. Amateur teams with such exotic monikers as Excelsiors, Atlantics, Putnams and Eckfords had of course played there as far back as 1849, and a loosely knit 24-team federation of East Coast teams that kicked off play in 1857 numbered no less than nine ball clubs representing Brooklyn borough neighborhoods. And these clubs were not without historical baseball distinction. It was the Eckfords who first paid an athlete (Al Reach) for his baseball services; the Excelsiors embarked on baseball's first extended road trip; the Brooklyn Stars featured hurler Candy Cummings who boasted the game's first curveball; and the Atlantics earned early baseball notoriety with an 1870 victory over Cincinnati's Red Stockings – baseball's first all-professional club – shattering the latter team's remarkable two-season 78-game unbeaten streak. The score was an undistinguished 8-7 in 10 innings, yet the result was perhaps the most famous ever recorded in the entire annals of amateur-league play.

But it was not until 1883 that the embryonic Dodgers emerged. This occurred when real estate executive and practicing attorney Charles H. Byrne, purportedly at the urging of *New York Herald* editor George Taylor, decided to invest capital in this promising new sport that was so rapidly becoming the craze of a booming industrial nation. Byrne, with financial backing from known gamblers Joe Doyle and Gus Abell, entered his new team in the short-lived Interstate League that year, having hurriedly constructed a makeshift ballpark on the very site where the nation's forefather, George Washington, had once fought a key Revolutionary War battle against the British. Entrenched in their new baseball park, Brooklyn's first "Dodgers" walked away with a pennant in that first and only season of Interstate League play.

Buoyed by such immediate success, Byrne next transferred his team to the more established American Association for the following season, an overly ambitious move which saw his club dashed from championship caliber to a ninth-place finish in the older 12-team circuit. While a lasting tradition of winning baseball was not born from these earliest seasons, a proud fixture of team identity was. It was in these first American Association years that the nickname "Dodgers" first came to common currency. Horse-drawn trolley cars comprised the early transportation network linking the numerous Dutch villages of which Brooklyn was composed. In an age of pedestrians, however, neighboring Manhattan residents had found this maze of carriages to be confusing and even life-threatening on occasion. Thus the disparaging appellation "Trolley Dodgers" was born. The nickname quickly stuck to common citizens of Brooklyn borough, as well as to the professional ball club that now represented borough pride. It continued for some time to share equal currency with more standard baseball nicknames such as Bridegrooms, Brooklyns, Brooklyners or simply Brooks.

Proud performances by the Brooklyn entry in the Interstate League of the early 1880s, and then in the much stronger American Association at the end of that decade, prompted Charles Byrne once again to transfer his Washington Park franchise to the even better situated National League in time for the 1890 spring season. And in one of the earliest ironic episodes surrounding the star-crossed Brooklyn team, the upstart Trolley Dodgers, managed by handsome moustachioed William McGunnigle and paced by right-handed hurler Bill "Adonis" Terry, romped to an easy pennant victory by six and a half lengths in their very first National League campaign. McGunnigle had also manufactured an earlier pennant for the Brooklyns during the final year of American Association play, but such successes were to matter little when front-office upheaval shook the club a scant season later and McGunnigle was dismissed after only three seasons at the helm.

The 1890 season – the first in Brooklyn's full-fledged major-league history – also witnessed less noble baseball endeavors. Formation of the abortive Players' League that same season, along with the inevitable ensuing bidding war for established baseball talent, left Brooklyn with teams in all three professional leagues that year (National League, Players' League and American Association), as well as stripping Byrne's Dodgers of some of their best talent and driving the two lesser leagues entirely out of business in the process. An ensuing shake-up of Brooklyn baseball personnel,

Several Daffy Dodger outfielders (left to right) – Jigger Statz, Rube Bressler, Harvey Hendrick, Ty Tyson, Babe Herman and Max Carey – pose in a late 1920s cameo. Tyson here places the year at 1928, which was the first of Herman's three incredible seasons at the plate, as he hit for averages of .340, .381 and .390 during those campaigns. This team finished in sixth place in 1928 under the guidance of "Uncle Robbie" – Wilbert Robinson.

Charles Ebbets reigned over the Brooklyn Baseball Club from the turn of the century until his death in early April, 1925. Ebbets' team began as Brooklyn's Trolley Dodgers. They were known for a time in the 1890s as Bridegrooms, then later as Hanlon's Superbas for manager Ned Hanlon.

which left Bill McGunnigle on the sidelines, ushered in John Montgomery Ward, drafted from the borough's Players' League entry, as McGunnigle's replacement. Ward was a colorful enough character – a longtime National League star shortstop and pitcher, eventual Hall of Famer, off-season distinguished lawyer who battled baseball's early reserve clause and was himself instrumental in the Players' League movement of 1890. Yet Ward proved far less successful as a big-league field boss. A sparseness of Brooklyn talent in the wake of the Players' League fiasco soon meant a succession of managerial replacements – Dave Foutz, William Barnie, Mike Griffen – all of whom did little to assuage sagging Brooklyn baseball fortunes throughout the remainder of the century's last decade.

Baseball progress is not measured by wins and losses alone, and the final decade of the nineteenth century was altogether significant in Brooklyn annals for matters transcending the team's dearth of on-field successes. The 1890s also witnessed the rise to power of the borough's first remarkable baseball personality. Charles Hercules Ebbets, an intelligent, affable and ambitious young businessman who came into the employment of Charles Byrne and his partners in 1894, was shortly to leave his indelible mark on Brooklyn baseball history. But Ebbets' steady rise to power with the Dodgers was often slow and painstaking during his earliest years with the club.

Brooklyn's first National League campaign in 1890 brought one further historic event worthy of passing mention – the first "intra-city" National League match-up of those storied rivals, the Dodgers and Giants. What was later to become the most fabled rivalry in all sports actually began as mere "inter-city" combat, rather than as

the celebrated "intra-city" contest which emerged only after New York's annexation of Brooklyn (still an independent municipality in 1890) after 1898. But from the first encounter of 1890, the Dodgers-Giants rivalry proved heated enough. Brooklyn was to win that first historic National League game 7-3, in old, original Washington Park before a meager attendance of only 3774, yet the stage was now set for intense inter-city games which would soon be drawing overflow crowds into the city's two major-league parks.

But just as the great rivalry of Dodgers and Giants was eventually to follow from East Coast to West, this first 1890 contest also marked a transfer of Brooklyn-New York combat from inter-league to intra-league play. As American Association champs in 1889, Brooklyn had already faced the National League champion Giants once before, the previous fall. In this preliminary World Series of sorts, Brooklyn had again won the opening meeting, 12-10, at the Polo Grounds. This first contest resulted in a donnybrook terminated by darkness and confusion befitting many Dodgers-Giants slugfests of decades to come. Nightfall descended, players stalled and umpires refused to halt play, but fans finally took matters into their own hands by storming the field and thus bringing the day's play to a halt. Three of the first four games of that bitter series ended in similar fashion – with crowds storming the field and ending play before nine official innings transpired, yet the proud Giants of New York were able to rebound from three defeats in those first four games to sweep the final five contests and take the series.

One of the more memorable events from the early tenure of Charles Ebbets with the Brooklyn club was a business transaction now somewhat hard to fathom in the frame of modern-day baseball management. Ebbets had already been a loyal employee with the Brooklyn club for six years by the time the Bridegrooms joined the National League; he sold scorecards and tickets, cleaned the grandstands and the club offices, and kept most of the financial ledgers as well. He even took over as field manager for the hapless ball club for part of the 1898 season, when the tenth-place Bridegrooms reached rock bottom in their tailspin of the late 1890s.

While making himself indispensable in the front office, Ebbets also shrewdly purchased whatever available club stock his limited resources would allow. By 1897, though owning only 10 percent of the club at the time, Charles Ebbets was elected team president, being acknowledged by his fellow owners (Byrne and his various shady associates) as the only knowledgeable base-ball man in the organization. And it was in the following season that his baseball acumen and business guile conspired to pull off a first blockbuster deal designed to radically transform Brooklyn baseball fortunes. Although his Baltimore Orioles were the unrivaled league champions of the period (pennant winners in 1894-1896), owner Harry Von der Horst (a Baltimore brewer with little real baseball interest) had enjoyed little success with his club at the gate. The crafty Ebbets, aware of Von der Horst's flagging interest, conspired to transfer majority ownership of the financially successful Brooklyn team to Von der Horst as well. League rules did not prevent multiple team ownership in those days. To the delight of Brooklyn rooters (and the immense satisfaction of the devious Ebbets), Von der Horst was then persuaded to enhance his new investment by shipping a cartload of his best Baltimore players to Brooklyn, along with crack manager Ned Hanlon to boot. Paced by ex-Orioles Wee Willie Keeler, Hughie Jennings, Joe Kelley, Joe "Iron Man" McGinnity and Jimmy Sheckard, the transformed Hanlon-led Brooklyn team predictably swept to easy pennants in both 1899 and 1900.

Hanlon's Baltimore-flavored Brooklyn team was like a momentary supernova, launched at the end of the National League's own brief monopoly on professional baseball. In 1901 a rival American League was put in place and the new eight-club circuit immediately set to work raiding rosters of the established National League rivals, as the Players' League had done a decade earlier. No club was more damaged by the crossfire than Brooklyn, with outfield standouts Keeler and Kelley and pitching stars McGinnity and Wild Bill Donovan immediately jumping to the new, high-paying league. Ned Hanlon's teams soon tumbled to fifth (1903), sixth (1904), and eighth (1905), losing 105 games in his final season of 1905 and finishing 56 and a half games behind the pace-setting World Champion Giants. That the rival New Yorkers had emerged as baseball's newest powerhouse under John J. McGraw, while Ned Hanlon's Superbas (formerly the Bridegrooms) stumbled to the league's basement, was particularly galling to the hordes of Brooklyn faithful.

Yet Charles Ebbets himself had little reason to grieve excessively. Ebbets had finally bought out Von der Horst with borrowed funds in 1904 and now was virtually sole owner of the ball club. He had immediately reelected himself club president, simultaneously raising his own salary from $4000 to $10,000 and cutting that of his field manager from $11,500 to $7500. By the conclusion of the disastrous 1905 campaign the disgruntled Hanlon had already departed and Wild Bill Donovan's brother, Patsy Donovan, was quickly appointed the new Brooklyn skipper for the 1906 season.

Brooklyn's fortunes continued to dip noticeably during the post-Hanlon years — two fifth-place finishes and a seventh-place season under Donovan; a single sixth-place campaign with Harry Lumley at the helm in 1909; two sixth-place years and two

Rube Marquard was on the down side of his 201-177 big-league career when he first arrived in Brooklyn for the 1916-1920 campaigns, but he did manage to record 19 victories in 1917. The Hall of Fame lefty's 19 consecutive victories for the Giants in 1912 are his lasting claim to baseball immortality. Marquard was 56-48 overall for Brooklyn.

seventh-place finishes under ex-shortstop Bill Dahlen between 1910 and 1913. A National League MVP season by first baseman Jack Daubert, who hit at a .350 clip in 1913, provided a rare uplift to the sagging Brooklyn fortunes. Yet Ebbets was well occupied at this time, about to hatch his grandest scheme yet – the one which would leave his most enduring mark on the Brooklyn baseball franchise that had become his personal fosterchild. Having

Right: *Lefty Jake Daubert was a heavy-hitting first baseman who became Brooklyn's first batting champ and first National League MVP, capturing both honors in 1913. Daubert also repeated as the league's leading hitter in 1914 with a .329 average, completing his 15-season big-league career at .303.*

Below: *Brooklyn manager Wilbert Robinson (far right) and his players gather at home plate to dispute a close call involving Jack Daubert (here bending over plate). This action occurred in the 1916 World Series against the Boston Red Sox. A remarkable Boston pitching staff featuring Babe Ruth, Ernie Shore, Dutch Leonard and Carl Mays shut down Brooklyn 4-1 in the first-ever Ebbets Field World Series.*

moved his club by 1898 into a new, 12,000-seat, wooden stadium, renamed Washington Park and located in south Brooklyn (they had played in Eastern Park since abandoning the original Washington Park in 1891), Ebbets had for some time longed for a still larger park with more seats and better control over paying customers. As the natural rivalry with McGraw's cross-town Giants heated up, regularly drawing huge crowds after the turn of the century, Ebbets was acutely aware of the financial boon represented by a new stadium. He especially wanted one that would prevent further freeloading by the Washington Park fans who, disgruntled with the team's diminished talents, preferred free vantage points atop the surrounding tenements to paid admissions (at a mere 50 cents a ticket) in the increasingly empty ballpark bleachers.

Again borrowing heavily in order to purchase a desired parcel of land near the outskirts of Flatbush – smack within the shantytown area known quaintly to locals as "Pigtown" – Ebbets successfully constructed his colossus of a ballpark in the nick of time for the opening of the 1913 season. The cost was steep, a quite considerable sum of $750,000 was invested in the new ballpark. It was an impressive edifice indeed – perhaps the finest in the major leagues – constructed of brick with great arched ornamental windows and a basilica-like rotunda entrance. Seating was available for 18,000, and a total capacity of 21,000 was possible with standees. On April 9, 1913, Ebbets Field first opened to a rain-diminished crowd of 12,000, in attendance to witness an inaugural loss by 1-0 to the Philadelphia Phillies. The unsung hero of this first Ebbets Field game was none other than Brooklyn's Casey Stengel. The young outfielder provided the Flatbush faithful with one genuine thrill for the otherwise dreary afternoon – a spectacular, first-inning, left-field catch which nearly saved the day for hard-luck Brooklyn southpaw Nap Rucker.

The financial arrangement which made possible the glorious new ballpark in Flatbush was, however, to have severe consequences for the next several generations of Brooklyn baseball management. Its fallout was still being felt, in fact, right down to the days of Branch Rickey at the dawn of the Jackie Robinson era. Ebbets had actually located his preferred site for the new ballpark as early as 1908, yet it took four years to obtain title to the entire four-and-a-half acre tract, and when construction of the ballpark began in 1912 the scheming Brooklyn owner was again strapped for cash. To finance construction of his new baseball home, Ebbets was forced to relinquish a full 50 percent of his holdings in the club to Brooklyn contractors Edward J. and Stephen W. McKeever. In return the affluent brothers infused the project with a much-needed $100,000 cash investment.

The new partnership resulted in two makeshift corporations, Brooklyn Baseball Club, Inc., with Ebbets as president and the senior Ed McKeever as vice-president, and the Ebbets-McKeever Exhibition Company (owner and operator of the ballpark facility), with Ed McKeever installed as president and Ebbets holding down the vice-president post. Steve McKeever served as treasurer of both companies, and while the ballpark operation ran smoothly enough under this arrangement, operation of the team was quite another matter. With the sudden death of Charlie Ebbets in the spring of 1925, followed almost immediately by that of Ed McKeever (who contracted pneumonia at Ebbets' funeral and succumbed a mere week later), the younger McKeever was to make his own grab for the privilege of ownership, ushering in a period of front-office stalemate, and a decade and a half of constant bickering between the McKeever and Ebbets interests in the faltering ball club.

If Ebbets Field had been the foremost legacy of Charles Ebbets' nearly 30 years at the helm of the Dodgers, the event of second greatest impact was his selection of the jovial Wilbert Robinson to direct the team's on-field fortunes. Robinson, who had once starred as a catcher for Baltimore's Orioles of the 1890s and still holds a century-old big-league record for seven hits in seven at-bats during a single game, became the new Brooklyn manager at the outset of the second season of play in Ebbets Field. Wilbert Robinson and Charles Ebbets were almost an ideal complementary pair to guide Brooklyn baseball fortunes in the period between the two world wars. The stuffy Squire of Brooklyn, as Ebbets was widely known, was time and again offset by the rotund, mild-mannered 51-year-old and long-time friend of ex-Baltimore sidekick John Muggsy McGraw. Robinson's well-established baseball image was, in fact, that of the consummate peace-maker, a role he had played while teammate to the irascible McGraw in Baltimore and then again as McGraw's trusty coach and advisor with the Giants. Only an irreparable split between Robinson and McGraw brought on by a bitter quarrel during the 1913 World Series gave Ebbets the opportunity to seize the talented and immensely popular Robinson for his own, and inflict a small wound upon the hated McGraw and his Giants in the process. Robinson, in turn, managed to

bring the Brooklyn team two pennants in his first seven seasons under Ebbets, a much welcomed improvement for a franchise that had not enjoyed victory since the 1900 campaign.

By the time the excessively good-natured Robinson was forced out of his managerial post almost two full decades later, Ebbets Field would be a venerable National League fixture more than twice the size of its original structure, the Daffiness Dodgers of the 1930s would be in full flower, and baseball would be standing on the doorstep of the modern radio and television age. Robinson's early years were promising enough. The 1916 club, buoyed by a third-place 1915 finish and the acquisition of pitchers Jack Coombs from the Athletics (for whom he had won 30 games a few seasons earlier), spitballing Larry Cheney from the Cubs, and left-hander Rube Marquard from the Giants, held on through the summer for a scant two-and-a-half game pennant margin over the Phillies, themselves paced by Grover Cleveland Alexander's spectacular 33 victories. While the 1916 team was quickly dispatched four games to one by the Red Sox and Babe Ruth in Brooklyn's first World Series appearance, the 1920 club under Uncle Robbie rebounded from three disastrous wartime years (seventh in 1917 and fifth the following two campaigns) and raced to a comfortable seven-game final margin over runner-up New York.

This time around the Brooklyns were confident of World Series victory against the opposition, which happened to be a heavy-hitting Cleveland club, led by play-

Wilbert Robinson (at right) and hurler Jack Coombs chat on the Ebbets Field sideline in August of 1916. Coombs won 13 games for the first-place Brooks that year, Robbie's first title in his third year at the helm. Robbie is today most remembered as a Falstaffian figure of considerable baseball acumen who presided season after season over an understaffed roster of hopeless losers in Brooklyn.

Above: *Zack Wheat scores Brooklyn's lone tally in the first game of the 1920 World Series against Cleveland, at Ebbets Field. Hall of Famer Wheat's finest all-around performance came during the Robins' pennant-winning campaign of 1916, a year when he hit .312 and ran off a 29-game batting streak eventually stopped by Cincinnati hurler Fred Toney. Wheat's only NL batting title was something of a bizarre footnote to baseball history, however, coming in the war-shortened 1918 campaign and resulting as much from a front-office executive ruling as from events on the field. Wheat played more seasons (18) than any other Dodger.*

ing-manager Tris Speaker with his robust .388 batting average and league-leading 50 doubles. Yet the 1920 Series, this time played under the experimental five-of-nine format instituted at the outset of World War I, again proved disheartening for Brooklyn, the final tally being five games to two in favor of the Indians. Ace spitballer Stan Coveleski shut out Brooklyn three times, only Zack Wheat (.333) and short-stop Ivy Olsen (.320) hit with any consistency for Uncle Robbie's men, and Burleigh Grimes provided the solitary bright spot for Brooklyn by shutting down Cleveland without a run in the second Series game.

The real story of the 1920 World Series, however, was the remarkable fifth game, played in Cleveland's League Park on October 10, and won handily 8-1 by the American League Indians. This single game – one of the most unforgettable in Series history – saw two unprecedented "firsts" and one spectacular "only" which more than spiced the day's play. In inning one Elmer Smith of Cleveland connected against Brooklyn ace Burleigh Grimes for the first ever World Series grand-slam homer. Not to be outdone, Cleveland hurler Jim Bagby (31-12 that season) touched Grimes as well for a three-run shot in inning three, the first homer by a pitcher in World Series play. But both hits were obscured for future generations by what transpired the following inning. With

Robins hugging each base, pitcher Clarence Mitchell was allowed by Uncle Robbie to bat for himself and promptly answered his skipper's faith by lining a screamer toward center field. What happened next stunned all in attendance, as Mitchell's apparent hit was miraculously speared by Indians second baseman Bill Wambsganss. Wamby reached instant immortality by converting Mitchell's smash into the only unassisted triple play in World Series annals. It is only an amusing footnote to this memorable moment that in Mitchell's next at-bat that day the Brooklyn spitballer also lined into a double play, thus becoming perhaps the only man in baseball history to account for five outs with just two swings of his impotent bat.

The final years of Uncle Robbie's reign ushered in unprecented front office bickering, accompanied by new low points in the on-field fortunes of the struggling Brooklyn ball club. A close second-place finish behind McGraw's Giants in 1924 was the only bright spot in a decade which brought six sixth-place finishes during seven futile seasons. This was the era of the Daffy Dodgers, when the only highlights were zany, on-field escapades and the lowlights were an ongoing series of hopeless front office stalemates.

With the sudden deaths of Ebbets and McKeever, the two factions controlling the ball club were each left holding exactly 50 percent of the stock and corresponding voting rights. While 70-year-old Steve McKeever coveted the team presidency for himself, the only acceptable compromise seemed to be the popular and harmless Uncle Robbie. Robinson was always a team man and reluctantly assumed the president's role alongside his managerial duties during the 1925 season. But deteriorating relations with Steve McKeever – who was further aggravated by Robinson's indelicate handling of the Brooklyn press – soon forced the disillusioned Wilbert Robinson to shun his executive office at Ebbets Field altogether and conduct what little business got done from his lonely clubhouse isolation. The bitter standoff continued right up until Robinson's removal as president in 1929 and his subsequent dismissal as manager in 1931. John Heydler, president of the National League, having grown tired of rapid deteriorations in Brooklyn's team management, intervened at long last with a series of compromise actions which spelled Uncle Robbie's eventual demise. Foremost of these was appointment of league representative Walter "Dutch" Carter as new Brooklyn board member, and it was Carter who eventually broke the deadlock and voted for Robinson's ouster. It was Carter as well who dictated that his own personal choice, Max Carey, was to be brought in as the new Brooklyn skipper in 1932.

The Robinson years did witness some of the most colorful and talented ballplayers ever to wear the Brooklyn uniform, as well as some of the most storied events of Brooklyn baseball lore. Zack Wheat amassed Brooklyn's longest playing career, hitting over .300 in 13 different seasons and enjoying two consecutive .375 seasons in 1923 and 1924. While toiling for weak-hitting Brooklyn teams between 1907 and 1916 and compiling an unimpressive lifetime mark of 134-134, Nap Rucker is today considered perhaps the finest natural left-hander ever to pitch for Brooklyn. The hard-luck Rucker once won 22 games for a 1911 Brooklyn ball club that amassed only 64 season victories. Babe Herman was, for all his defensive shortcomings, perhaps the finest natural hitter ever to put on the Brooklyn colors, enjoying a remarkable 1930 campaign in which he batted .393 (an all-time franchise standard) and drove home 130 runs. Dazzy Vance and Burleigh Grimes provided Brooklyn with the league's most intimidating pitching duo of the 1920s, with Vance leading the league twice in games won and Grimes winning 20 on four different occasions.

It was ultimately the colorful exploits of the 1920s Dodgers as bumbling baseball showmen that most distinguished the Wilbert Robinson chapter of Brooklyn baseball history. Robinson was a man always dogged by unusual events and blessed – or cursed – by high-spirited players. Even visiting teams brought zaniness to Ebbets Field during Robinson's long tenure. But Uncle Robbie had himself early set the tone for high-jinks, attempting to catch a baseball dropped from a circling biplane during spring training of 1916. This particular incident ended with appropriate embarrassment for the proud manager when the falling sphere turned out to be a grapefruit (supplied by the puckish Stengel) which splattered all over the panicked ex-catcher, convincing him momentarily that his own head had been split open in the process.

But among the hordes of Brooklyn faithful, the true moniker for their beloved charges was never really plain "Dodgers" anyway, even after Uncle Robbie's departure from the Brooklyn baseball scene in 1932. That honor belongs to a popular label that had already stuck to the club in press column and grandstand alike during the earliest Depression years. For most Flatbush rooters of the final three Brooklyn decades, the Dodgers were universally accepted simply as "Dem Loveable Bums" – an image so endearing to Brooklyn fans that even the sober Walter O'Malley was loathe to lobby against it during the final Brooklyn years. "Bums" – as earlier Dodgers historians have hastened to recount – was an improbable nickname that itself entails a rich baseball legend worthy of retelling here.

Contemporary newspaper accounts have it that a certain Brooklyn diehard of the Depression era took special pleasure in loudly bemoaning the inept play of the local team from his safe but clearly audible refuge in the box seats behind home plate. This leather-lunged fan held sway for

Below: Babe Herman (seen here in 1931) looms from the 1930s as baseball's own original free spirit, famed for bone-headed play; and yet for a few seasons (hitting .381 in 1929 and .393 in 1930, yet failing to win any batting titles) he was also without peer as a dauntless National League slugger. No incident of Herman's illustrious career better capsulizes the charm of the Daffy Dodgers than the one which transpired on a sleepy summer afternoon of 1926, when Brooklyn's Babe (with the aid of an equally inept third base coach) ran a booming double into an unexpected double play. This was the infamous moment that found three Dodgers simultaneously hugging third base. What almost always goes without mention about this amusing moment is the fact that Herman's blast to center that day also delivered the game-winning run against Boston.

Right-handed ace hurler Burleigh Grimes demonstrates his infamous spitball. A distinguishing feature of Grimes, who pitched in Brooklyn from 1918 to 1926, was a temper and disposition as mean as his feared fastball. Grimes often feuded with teammates and opponents alike, and he sported a reputation among the league's batsmen as an altogether terrifying hurler to face. Old Stubblebeard won 270 games in his 19-year Hall of Fame career, and of 17 established spitball pitchers allowed to continue their trade when "wet ones" were outlawed in 1920, Grimes hung around the longest.

several seasons with one particular favorite epithet – "Ya bum, ya" – usually directed generously at each and every member of the Brooklyn team. Local baseball writer Sid Mercer was especially taken with this boisterous rooter – he even dubbed him "the spirit of Brooklyn" – and picked up the popular local expletive in his daily reportage of Dodgers games. "Bums Win" or "Bums Lose" was soon a familiar enough sight on the sports pages of the *Brooklyn Eagle.*

But it remained for New York sports cartoonist Willard Mullin to create the endearing, pudgy hobo, with his characteristic cigar stub, bearded chin, and tattered jacket, that was eventually to become the unofficial Dodgers logo before the onset of World War II. Walter O'Malley, always able to recognize a good marketing gimmick when he saw one, eventually even employed Mullin to draw his popular, sleazy mascot for the covers of team yearbooks and press guides. Like no other professional baseball club before or since, the Dodgers of Brooklyn were a true team of the people – a community institution for which nearly every local citizen felt the deepest passion. There is a certain fitting poignancy, therefore, to the fact that it was the fans of Brooklyn themselves who would ultimately honor their team with a most fitting identity – one all of their own choosing.

The remaining years of the 1930s saw three talented yet star-crossed managers try vainly to lift the entertaining but ultimately hapless Dodgers out of a decade of second-division play. Max Carey (1932-1933), Casey Stengel (1934-1936), and Burleigh Grimes (1937-1938) took turns at trying to right the Brooklyn fortunes, yet each met with similar failures. Carey enjoyed the most productive campaign, a third-place finish in 1932; neither Stengel nor Grimes posted a single winning mark nor a finish higher than fifth. But the standard for daffy play which reached its height in the final seasons under Wilbert Robinson maintained its course under his three successors as well. Stengel in particular was blessed with a continuation of Dodger daffiness to which Casey himself contributed in ample measure, assisted by such memorable characters as outfielder Frenchy Bordagaray, streaky hitter Len Koenecke, and intemperate slugger Hack Wilson. Bordagaray reputedly once gave up on a fly ball against the Cubs to chase his wind-blown cap instead. Another famous incident involves Hack Wilson suffering through a gigantic hangover on a sunny afternoon in Philadelphia's Baker Bowl. Dodgers hurler Walter "Boom Boom" Beck, distraught about being removed from the mound that day by manager Stengel, refused to hand Casey the ball and instead whirled and threw the offending sphere high against the right-field fence. Wilson, at that moment lost in private thought while squinting at the grass before him, whirled suddenly, seized the caroming baseball, and threw a perfect strike to third base, well ahead of the phantom runner.

The expected departure of manager Burleigh Grimes after the 1938 season ironically opened the door for the long-awaited first decade of sustained baseball success in Brooklyn franchise history. And the primary authors of that success were a rampaging innovative general manager and the fireplug field manager who was to be his first and most remarkable front office acquisition. Under pioneering general manager Larry MacPhail and dugout general Leo "The Lip" Durocher, the Dodgers wasted little time launching a decade of baseball triumphs that would end forever Brooklyn's long-standing image of impossible losers and incorrigible baseball clowns.

The long-awaited transition in Brooklyn baseball fortunes did not come, however, without considerable pressure from outside forces. Nearly a decade and a half of feuding for control of the organization, precipitated by Charles Ebbets' sudden death in 1925, had left the Brooklyn organization on the brink of destruction. By the close of the 1937 season, National League president Ford Frick – fearing the possible demise of one of the circuit's oldest and once most stable ball clubs – intervened and urged that Brooklyn ownership employ fresh blood in the front office. Frick's nominee for

such a role was Leland Stanford MacPhail, a Branch Rickey protege who had most recently run the Cincinnati club for Powell Crosley. MacPhail had already amply established his phenomenal front office skills while in Cincinnati, turning around an almost moribund ball club in a few short seasons and pioneering with such baseball firsts as the advent of major-league night baseball and the commercial radio broadcasting of Cincinnati home ball games.

MacPhail was quick to bring these same innovations to Brooklyn, employing his honey-voiced Cincinnati broadcaster, Walter (Red) Barber, to broadcast the first games from Ebbets Field, and scheduling as well the first New York City night game at Ebbets Field in June of 1938. MacPhail – a genius for crowd-promoting gimmicks – also hired Babe Ruth as his Dodgers first base coach and batting instructor. While Ruth lasted only one season and was himself bitterly disappointed at not being considered for a managerial slot at the conclusion of 1938, his brief appearance in Brooklyn did bring hordes of fans out to the grandstand to watch the Babe take batting practice and crush line drives on to nearby Bedford Avenue. MacPhail also occupied his first season in Brooklyn with acquiring hitting talent that would change the course of Dodgers history within a few short seasons. Batting star Dolph Camilli was purchased from the Phillies for $50,000; future fan-favorite Fred "Dixie" Walker was obtained on waivers from the Tigers in July 1939; a young jewel from the St. Louis Cardinals' farm system, promising outfielder "Pistol Pete" Reiser, was plucked from free agency (imposed by Commissioner Ford Frick) for an almost laughable $100 bonus; Harold "Pee Wee" Reese was similarly stolen from the Boston Red Sox organization early in 1940; and slugging star Joe Medwick was acquired from the Cardinals as well in 1940. Medwick, however, was soon severely injured when beaned by St. Louis hurler Bob Bowman a mere week after the trade, and never proved the valuable outfield addition the Dodgers and MacPhail had hoped.

MacPhail was a considerable breath of fresh air for Brooklyn and New York baseball. The new Dodgers boss spent several thousand dollars in renovation of Ebbets Field, painting and repairing the well-worn grandstand, and refurbishing restroom and clubhouse facilities. His decision to send home games out over the radio airwaves in 1938 was a stroke of genius. The move broke a long-standing gentleman's agreement between the three New York clubs not to provide free radio access to locally played games, and thus launched the age of

regular radio baseball broadcasts in the nation's largest city. MacPhail's dismissal of Grimes as manager and his simultaneous promotion of shortstop Leo Durocher to the bench for the opening of the 1939 campaign began a new era of Dodger success at the outset of the 1940s. That success was quickly realized with a near-pennant in 1940 and the team's first league title in 21 seasons the following year.

But it was MacPhail's introduction of night baseball that provided the final highlight moment of the 1930s and gave witness to one of the most remarkable events in all Dodger history. Fan response to the first Ebbets Field night game on June 15, 1938 – played against MacPhail's former club, the Cincinnati Reds – was so overwhelming that fire marshalls had to close the gates to further admissions several hours before actual game time. MacPhail's circus-like pre-game events were highlighted by an exhibition footrace featuring recent Olympic hero Jesse Owens. Enhancing the special atmosphere of the evening was the fact that Reds starting hurler, left-hander Johnny Vander Meer, was fresh off a masterful no-hit performance against the Boston Braves only four nights earlier. History was on MacPhail's side that night, and under the influence of Brooklyn's new archlights, Vander Meer became the first and only pitcher in baseball's entire history to pitch a second consecutive no-hit game. A new era of nightime baseball had opened under MacPhail with perhaps the most famous game ever played in the 44-year history of storied Ebbets Field.

Above: *A unique view from the left-field stands during one of Ebbets Field's most historic games. The date is June 15, 1938, and the first night game ever in Brooklyn is underway. The Cincinnati Reds are the opponents and Johnny Vander Meer is in the process of achieving baseball immortality as he hurls a second consecutive no-hit game in a 6-0 whitewashing of Brooklyn. It was ironically from Cincinnati that GM Larry MacPhail had brought the notion of night-time baseball, which proved a huge success in the years immediately preceding World War II. Note the packed grandstands and the photographers clustered along the first base line as Vander Meer starts his delivery from the mound.*

2. Wartime Dodgers– From Hurricane Larry to Rickey and Robinson

The 1940s was a decade in which the face of professional baseball was changed forever by events both internal and external to the nation's pastime. The outbreak of World War II in December 1941 meant loss of the bulk of hearty major leaguers to military conscription, as well as wartime travel restrictions and material shortages which impacted heavily upon the game as well. Baseball also faced further manpower problems while the war raged on across Pacific and European theaters: the Mexican League made severe player-raiding forays into both the American and National Leagues in 1946; ownership soon faced a nearly successful organization of the much-feared players' union; and by the close of the decade the game had opened up to both blacks and Hispanics for the first time in the present century. Air travel began to replace train travel, and increased radio coverage of big-league games was followed at war's end with the first glimmer of televised baseball. And night baseball had become an established practice by the close of the decade as well.

In National League ballparks two great ball clubs were also busy establishing their domination over the sport in this new age of rapid technological change and social upheaval. The St. Louis Cardinals, reaping the bounteous harvest of an elaborate farm system cultivated by Branch Rickey throughout the 1930s, captured four pennants and three World Series, while also finishing second five times between 1941 and 1949. And in Brooklyn, the newly constructed Dodgers, put in place by Larry MacPhail at the close of the previous decade, also emerged as a potent force, winning three pennants and grabbing three second-place finishes as well. Only 1945 (Cubs) and 1948 (Braves) saw anything but Cardinal and Dodger domination of the senior circuit during the remainder of the decade.

Foundations for the great Brooklyn Dodgers teams of the 1940s and early 1950s were carefully laid in place by Hurricane Larry MacPhail just before the outbreak of the war years in late 1941. Pee Wee Reese, Pete Reiser, Dolph Camilli, and the popular Fred "Dixie" Walker, universally known to the Brooklyn fans (in quaint Brooklynese) as The Peepul's Cherce, were among the major MacPhail acquisitions of 1939 and 1940. Camilli socked 34 homers and drove home 120 runs, both league-leading totals, in 1941. Walker hit .308 and .311 in his first two Brooklyn seasons, while Reiser paced the National League in batting (.343 in

Fred "The People's Cherce" Dixie Walker strikes a classic batting pose. From deep in rural Georgia, Walker was to remain an Ebbets Field crowd favorite, from his arrival from Detroit in 1939 until his departure to the Pirates in 1948. A heavy hitting lefty, Walker paced the National League in batting in 1944 (.357) and in RBIs (124) the following summer. His 18-year career with five teams resulted in a respectable .306 career average. Yet Walker is perhaps best remembered for his 1947 demand that he be traded rather than play on the same team with Jackie Robinson. Though he would later recant and publicly admit Robinson's positive impact on the team's pennant fortunes in 1947, the damage was done and Walker was unhappily shipped away before 1948 had ended.

1941) and stolen bases (twice, with 20 in 1942 and 34 in 1946) before injuries halted his promising career. Reese was to become a mainstay of Dodger teams through most of the next two decades.

But one such deal went quickly sour for the usually crafty franchise builder who had taken over the Dodgers front office only months before the death of club president Steve McKeever. On June 12, 1940, Mac-Phail announced his most startling deal of all, purchase of slugging St. Louis outfielder Joe "Ducky" Medwick, along with side-arming pitcher Curt Davis, for four players and the then-huge sum of $125,000 cash. Medwick was a true superstar, having led the league in RBI totals thrice (1936-1938) as well as in homers (31 in 1937) during immediately preceding seasons. At age 28 the slugging future Hall of Famer was certainly anything but washed up. But Medwick's star was ill-fated in Brooklyn from the start, and his rapid downward spiral began with his first game in Brooklyn flannels. With the Cardinals in town only a week after the Medwick deal was announced, St. Louis hurler Bob Bowman struck the new Dodger slugger with a vicious beanball, triggering a bench-clearing brawl between the two heated rivals. Howls of protest arose from Dodger manager Durocher, who had reason enough to believe the incident was premeditated. Bad blood had long stood between Bowman and ex-Cardinal Durocher, and a pre-game incident reportedly had Medwick and Durocher needling Bowman in a hotel elevator only hours before the ill-fated encounter. Medwick, at any rate, was hospitalized for a week and upon his return to the Brooklyn lineup seemingly had lost forever the aggressive posture which had heretofore made him one of the league's outstanding batters. Medwick did hit slightly over .300 for most of the next three seasons before the Dodgers finally dispatched him to the Giants in 1944, but he hit less than 30 Brooklyn home runs and never did justify MacPhail's hefty investment. Durocher and MacPhail, meanwhile, protested vehemently to league president Ford Frick, demanding a lifetime ban for Bowman. The protest only fell on deaf ears, however, as did MacPhail's subsequent attempts to have the villainous Cardinal hurler indicted by civil authorities on a charge of attempted murder.

Of all MacPhail's astute moves in rebuilding the Dodgers ball club, none was more unanticipated than his surprise announcement at the close of the 1938 World Series that fireplug veteran shortstop Leo Durocher would replace longtime Dodger favorite Burleigh Grimes as field

Left: *Joe "Ducky" Medwick as a member of the St Louis Cardinals. Medwick never repaid the Dodgers' $125,000 investment after a June 1940 beaning robbed the heavy-hitting outfielder of much of his aggressive-style play.*

Below: *Leo Durocher in a familiar posture as he lives up to his lippy reputation. Leo here rushes to the field to protest umpire Bill McGowan's call of ball four to Giant batter Sid Gordon. Dodger pitcher Witlow Wyatt joins the heated exchange.*

Pee Wee Reese as a rookie in Spring Training, 1940. The "Little Colonel" from Ekron, Kentucky, will always be remembered as captain of "Boys of Summer" teams in the early and mid-1950s. A brash rookie at the height of Mr. MacPhail's tenure in 1940, Reese was still around for one brief season in Los Angeles in 1958. Only twice did he lead the NL in individual offensive categories (104 walks in 1947, and 132 runs in 1949), yet the diminutive shortstop was a perennial All-Star selection between 1947 and 1954. A consummate team player, Reese sacrificed his potential as a talented basestealer to the Dodgers' preferred hit-and-run style of play under Durocher, Shotton and Dressen.

general for the 1939 campaign. It was not that the demise of Grimes was itself entirely unexpected (his teams lost over 80 games both years he managed), but rather that the colorful Durocher would be deemed worthy as his replacement. Leo was already a household baseball figure of considerable reputation, especially as a more-than-competent shortstop for Branch Rickey's St. Louis Gas House Gang of the 1930s. Durocher had been reluctantly dealt away to the second division Dodgers by Rickey in 1937 only after the growing conflicts between Durocher and equally volatile Cardinal manager Frankie Frisch became too much for the St. Louis clubhouse to bear.

Durocher's cantankerous behavior of course transported to Brooklyn, and relationships between "Leo the Lip" and the "Roaring Redhead" MacPhail were to be at the near boiling point throughout MacPhail's Dodger tenure. MacPhail seemingly fired and rehired Durocher at whim — a half dozen times — during the next three seasons. And Durocher's career — one of the most colorful in baseball history — would remain as chaotic in the post-MacPhail years as well. Witness his equally stormy relationship with Branch Rickey during the remainder of the decade; ill-advised connections with gambling elements which caused a one-year baseball suspension in 1947; eight seasons and two pennants as

Giants manager after departing Brooklyn in 1948; a volatile marriage to actress Larraine Day and some well-touted show business connections which landed an undistinguished later career as television broadcaster; an eventual return to baseball, first as Los Angeles Dodgers coach and then as manager of the 1966-1972 Chicago Cubs; a belated conclusion to his illustrious 24-year managerial career with the Houston Astros in 1972-1974.

A first noticeable milestone for the resurrected Dodgers under Larry MacPhail was the season of 1940. That first summer of the new decade saw a more competitive Brooklyn team, but one still somewhat green in the heat of the final stretch drive by the powerful Cincinnati team. This was the same Cincinnati ball club, of course, which MacPhail had ironically built before quarrelling with Reds owner Powell Crosley. Cincinnati had raced to a four-and-a-half game season-final lead over Rickey's Cardinals in 1939, and paced by 20-game winners Bucky Walters and Paul Derringer, the Reds were again easy winners (by a full 12 games) this time around over the upstart Dodgers. Yet Brooklyn astonished by winning 88 games under Durocher in 1940. Medwick and Camilli paced the hitting attack, ranking third and fourth in the league in total bases. Veteran pitcher Witlow Wyatt was league runner-up in strikeouts and tied for the lead in shutouts, while winning 15 games. Although never seriously challenging the powerful Cincinnati ball club after mid-summer, Brooklyn's second-place finish nonetheless rejuvenated most ardent Dodgers supporters, this being the best showing the team had mustered since the remote campaign of 1924.

The 1941 pennant race allowed the first glimpse of full blown Dodger successes to come. The summer of 1941 demonstrated surprising maturity in young players like Reese and Reiser, and the joyous result was an unexpected pennant for Brooklyn under third-year manager Leo Durocher. Reiser (the league's youngest batting leader ever, at age 22) and Camilli (home run king and RBI champion, as well as league MVP) were the offensive stalwarts, while MacPhail's latest acquisition, fastballer Kirby Higbe from the Phillies, tied Witlow Wyatt with a league-leading 22 victories. Reiser and Wyatt trailed Camilli by only a handful of votes for National League MVP honors. The pennant race was a nailbiter right down to the wire, with the Brooklyns edging out the rival Cardinals by two and a half games in what was a strictly two-team race almost from the opening bell. On September 25th, with but three games to play,

Wyatt shut down the Braves in Boston and the Dodgers had claimed their first pennant after an incredible dry spell of 21 years.

But even in the moment of victory the stormy personalities of MacPhail and Durocher managed to remain the featured Brooklyn baseball story. An exasperated MacPhail opened the team's public victory celebration in Grand Central Station that September by dramatically announcing one of Durocher's several firings for the season. This one resulted directly from the manager's refusal to let the team train stop at New York's 125th Street Station (he feared many of his players would jump ship) on its triumphant return from the pennant-clinching game in Boston. Mac-Phail, who had been planning to board at 125th Street and partake of his team's tumultuous celebration, was left rushing to Grand Central Station by taxi and vowing that Durocher this time was through for good. Later he relented somewhat and re-hired his repentant manager the following morning, but only after patiently hearing Durocher's own apologetic explanation of the incident.

If the summer of 1941 was a glorious time to sit in the bleachers of Ebbets Field and root for the triumphant Dodgers, the autumn of that same season was a time of diminished joy, bringing with it perhaps the darkest single moment in the long rollercoaster saga of Brooklyn baseball. For it is the 1941 World Series that will always be remembered for one inexcusable play, a

Club president Larry MacPhail (left) and manager Leo Durocher ride through the streets of Brooklyn on September 29, 1941, as the Dodgers celebrate their first NL Championship in 21 long years. Behind follow cars transporting the entire Brooklyn team. Rabid Dodger fans literally jam the streets on all sides as they turn the town over to their beloved "Bums," who are about to do battle for the first time with the crosstown rival New York Yankees in the World Series. The large sign above MacPhail's shoulder announces consensus support for skipper Durocher after his first pennant triumph in New York. Brooklyn hopes would soon enough be dashed in five short games, however, by the powerful Yankees of Dickey, DiMaggio and Keller.

Above: *Pete Reiser is carried from the field shortly after being injured in an August 1, 1946 game with the St. Louis Cardinals. Reiser had recklessly run into the left-field wall in an all-out attempt to snag Whitey Kurowski's long hit. Pete Reiser was baseball excitement two full decades before Pete Rose, providing power at the plate (leading the league with a .343 BA in 1941) and speed on the bases (league stolen-base champion in 1942 and 1946), but his near Hall of Fame career was cut off prematurely by a series of unfortunate injuries resulting from aggressive and uncontrolled play. Repeated outfield collisions and a serious 1941 beaning took their toll (as did three years of military service at the height of his career), and Reiser was through in 1952 after but 10 years of often brilliant big-league play.*

single bonehead moment which revived ghosts of hapless Brooklyn seasons past. Even Wambsganss's triple play in 1920 pales beside the World Series disaster which befell the Dodgers on October 5, 1941 – the only game in Series history to be won and lost after a batter actually struck out with two men already retired and his team trailing in the top of the ninth. The events of that nightmare afternoon would also serve to set the tone for a string of Brooklyn World Series disasters to be played out several times over the next decade and a half. It was game four in Ebbets Field, when Brooklyn's veteran catcher Mickey Owen unwittingly grabbed hold of baseball infamy by failing to maintain his grasp on one of reliever Hugh Casey's patented fast-balls. With the Dodgers leading 4-3 in the top of the ninth and two men already re-tired, Casey blazed strike three past Yankee mainstay Tommy Heinrich; unfortunately the pitch also eluded Owen and opened the floodgates for a four-run upris-ing that provided the New Yorkers with an insurmountable 3-1 Series lead. This moment was to live for a decade as the dark-est in Dodgers history – until Thomson's wallop against Branca at the Polo Grounds almost exactly 10 years later to the day.

Although the outbreak of war against Japan and Germany in late 1941 robbed the Dodgers of one key veteran player – in-fielder Cookie Lavagetto being the first Brooklyn player to join the war effort – the remainder of the squad stayed intact and the Dodgers appeared to be runaway repeat winners as they built up a 10-game lead over St. Louis by August of 1942. But the Cardinals were the supreme National League team throughout most of the decade, with sluggers Stan Musial, Enos Slaughter and Walker Cooper pacing their potent attack, and in the final months of

1942 St. Louis put on one of baseball's greatest finishes. League MVP Mort Cooper, with 22 victories and an incredible 1.77 ERA, was the pitching hero as St. Louis took 21 of 26 September games, 106 of the season, and bested the Dodgers by a scant two games. Brooklyn's 104 victories in 1942 set a club record, and yet they were insufficient to overcome a devastating in-jury which kayoed Pete Reiser in St. Louis during mid-July. Batting nearly .390 at the time, Reiser crashed into the outfield wall in hopeless pursuit of an Enos Slaughter home run ball, an episode which caused the brilliant Dodger outfielder to suffer dizzy spells, headaches and double vision throughout much of the remaining sum-mer. Reiser played erratically after July and slipped to a .310 batting average by sea-son's end. This tragic event – coupled with Leo Durocher's refusal to rest his star later in the season – brought a premature end to Pete Reiser's short career and robbed him of almost certain Hall of Fame credentials as well.

Larry MacPhail's own short but highly successful reign with the Dodgers also came to a sudden end at the conclusion of the 1942 campaign. It was in December of that year that MacPhail, stirred by the action overseas, resigned to accept a com-mission in the U.S. Army's Office of Service and Supply and thus became the first rank-ing baseball executive to cast his lot with the military effort. MacPhail was not done on the New York baseball scene of course; his return as Yankee general manager after the war was destined to embroil Yankees and Dodgers management in a Series of bitter confrontations before the end of the 1947 season. But MacPhail's legacy and contribution in Brooklyn was already beyond measure by the time of his unexpected 1942 departure. Ebbets Field had been refurbished and renovated for night baseball; adroit dealing had brought a bevy of players – Camilli, Medwick, Reiser, Wyatt, Higbie, Arky Vaughan, Billy Herman – who had finally lifted Brooklyn to the pinnacle of National League prominence; young talent like Reese, Lavagetto and Dixie Walker promised future Brooklyn successes for the remainder of the decade as well.

Yet for all the upswing in baseball for-tunes during MacPhail's Brooklyn reign, the McKeever and Ebbets heirs still in con-trol of the club were not entirely happy with financial matters. While $600,000 of debt to the Brooklyn Trust Company had been paid off and existing mortgages on the ballpark had been reduced considerably, most of the team's soaring profits had been poured back into player purchases and into a farm system resembling Mr. Rickey's model in St. Louis. MacPhail himself was drawing a princely salary, but ownership saw little likelihood of their own investments turning an appreciable business profit. Thus when MacPhail made known his plans for army enlistment the Board of Directors did little to dissuade him. Steve McKeever's son-in-law, Jim Mulvey, and Ebbets spokesman Joe Gilleaudeau were also acutely aware at the time that Branch Rickey, architect of those Cardinals teams which had proved such a Dodgers nemesis, had recently come to a bitter parting with St. Louis owner Sam Beardon. Rickey was promptly hired by the Dodgers governing board and given a five-year deal almost identical to the one under which MacPhail had operated for the previous half decade. "The Mahatma" – as New York sportswriter Tom Meany had affectionately tabbed him – had now arrived in Brooklyn, and baseball and the Dodgers would never be quite the same again.

With Brooklyn baseball fortunes now at a crucial crossroad, Dodgers executives had made a fateful decision in replacing Mac-Phail with a man so fully opposite of character, one who seemed destined to lift the Dodgers franchise to new and greater heights. While MacPhail was always forceful and often explosive, Rickey was a man of softspoken virtue and highest ideal. A deeply religious man who shunned the ball-

park on Sundays and never uttered a vain epithet beyond his trademark "Judas Priest!", Wesley Branch Rickey was also the shrewdest judge of young baseball talent the game has ever known. What was unanticipated in the spring of 1943, of course, was just how drastically this innovative executive would change baseball history forever during his short Brooklyn sojourn.

Rickey is today justifiably remembered almost exclusively for Jackie Robinson and baseball's noble integration experiment. But more significant to Brooklyn baseball fortunes, in reality, was the concept of an expansive farm system which he imported from his years in St. Louis. Rickey's style was to recruit virtually every promising teenager spotted by his extensive scouting organization, to sign eager youngsters for nothing but a pittance and the slim hope of someday making the big time, and then to select out the most exceptional talent through one of baseball's most exacting winnowing processes ever set in motion. The backbone of a Dodger team that was to win five pennants in the late 1940s and early 1950s was soon put carefully in place with the Old Mahatma's time-tested methods. That backbone included young Edwin "Duke" Snider, spotted as a California prep star; Gil Hodges, signed as a shortstop and later converted to a catcher before eventually assuming his destined

A panorama of Ebbets Field on May 8, 1942. A flag-raising ceremony launches the Navy Relief twilight exhibition game between the Dodgers and rival Giants, which was witnessed by an estimated 40,000 paying fans. Dodger players are seen lined up along the first base foul line, and the famous concave Ebbets Field right-field wall is here in full display.

spot at first base; Carl Furillo, the outfielder who played the first of his 15 years with the Dodgers in 1946, Carl Erskine, and an eventual host of black prospects as well, headlined by Robinson, Roy Campanella, and pitchers Joe Black and Dan Bankhead.

World War II temporarily derailed the Dodgers, as it did most other major-league teams of the early and mid-1940s. More than 60 percent of major-league personnel was to be found in military uniform by the 1944 and 1945 seasons, and big-league play was staffed largely by 4-F's (one-armed Pete Gray appeared with the Browns, and two epileptics held down infield spots with Cincinnati), overaged veterans (Pepper Martin returned to the Cardinals at age 40 after a four-year retirement), unprepared youngsters (15-year-old Joe Nuxhall took the mound for one game with the Reds and amassed a 67.50 season ERA), and the first tentative wave of Latin American players as well. With few bona fide major leaguers themselves, the Dodgers slipped to seventh in 1944, while maintaining third slot in 1943 and 1945. Durocher was still on the scene, having miraculously escaped the draft with a punctured eardrum, as was Dixie Walker, who personally salvaged something of 1944 with a National League batting title. Such undistinguished names as Alex Campanis (later Dodgers player personnel director), Gene Mauch (long-time big-league manager), Ed Basinski (an off-season concert violinist), and Tommy Brown (a 16-year-old interim shortstop),

attempted vainly to fill in for the departed Reese, Camilli, Lavagetto, Higbe, Reiser, Hugh Casey, Billy Herman, and other departed regulars lost temporarily to the war effort.

The first full post-war year of 1946 saw the Dodgers back on track. With peacetime optimism and a full complement of players returned to the big-league scene, a torrid pennant race unfolded in the National League that summer, one which found long-time rivals Brooklyn and St. Louis again locked in a dead heat on closing day. The unwanted result was the first post-season pennant playoff series in the history of the national pastime, a two-game affair swept by the red-hot St Louis Cardinals of manager Eddie Dyer.

But greatness was clearly on the horizon for the Dodgers, and 1946 was a season that seemed to vindicate Rickey's slow rebuilding process, so hampered by four previous seasons of wartime baseball. But this was also a season notable on several further counts. Jackie Robinson began his organized baseball career that summer for the Dodgers' International League affiliate in Montreal. Promising 24-year-old outfielder Carl Furillo was promoted to the parent club in Brooklyn and hit .284 his rookie campaign. Mexican millionaire Jorge Pascual launched his abortive plan aimed at enticing major-league talent to sign on for Mexican League play, plucking outfielder Luis Olmo and catcher Mickey Owen from the Dodgers. A short-lived players union movement failed to get off the ground but did set the stage for the full unionization of players that was eventually realized the following decade. And before a July 5th game at the Polo Grounds, Leo Durocher reportedly uttered his famous aphorism that "Nice guys finish last" – in response to a reporter's request for Leo's commentary on rival manager Mel Ott of the Giants.

The crown jewel of Rickey's all-too-brief tenure in Brooklyn was the championship 1947 season. That second post-war year has been immortalized in the hindsight of history, of course, as "the year all hell broke loose in baseball." Rickey launched his successful plan to tear apart baseball's long-standing policies of unjust racial prejudice. This season was without doubt dominated from start to finish by the story of Jackie Robinson's dramatic rookie season and baseball's hard-won campaign for true integration. But in Brooklyn this was also the dawn of the "Boys of Summer" Dodgers team that was destined to rule the National League for the next full decade.

Led by Robinson, baseball's first Rookie-of-the-Year selection, Brooklyn surged to its first pennant under the tempestuous partnership of Branch Rickey and Leo Durocher, a five-game bulge over the still pesky Cardinals that was never quite as close as the final margin would suggest. But the season was filled with drama enough – some of it transpiring even before spring training had ended and Robinson had appeared in his first tension-filled National League game. Brooklyn's season had started with a bang during spring training in Havana when skipper Durocher received a stunning suspension from Commissioner Happy Chandler. The charge was consorting with known gamblers and suspected criminal types. Baseball's extreme sanction of Durocher was to last for a season and was brought on in large part by an ongoing feud between the Dodgers' man-

ager and a familiar enough foe, his ex-boss Larry MacPhail. Now president and part owner of the Yankees, MacPhail was galled by earlier published barbs from Durocher and took the opportunity to protest successfully to the Commissioner about the Brooklyn manager's repeated underworld contacts.

The 1947 World Series was one of the most dramatic and inspired ever played. That the crosstown Yankees again prevailed in seven hard-fought games is but the barest outline of the story. Game four was the centerpiece, an "almost" first World Series no-hitter by journeyman New York pitcher Bill Bevens. But the ill-fated

Below left: *Jackie Robinson and Branch Rickey pose at a contract signing in February 1948 as the Dodgers' first Rookie of the Year renews for a second season.*

Below: *Robinson is seen here in the Ebbets Field dugout, signing autographs for young admirers on the historic day of his first big-league game, April 11, 1947.*

Bevens saw his dream of immortality shattered when a two-out ninth-inning double off the bat of pinch hitter Cookie Lavagetto brought home two crucial runs. Bevens, who had already walked 10 and given up an earlier run, had lost not only his masterpiece but the game (by the count of 3-2) in the process. Almost anticlimactic in the face of game four was Al Gionfriddo's unbelievable left-field grab the next day of DiMaggio's sinking line drive, a play that saved the day for Brooklyn and sent the Series to another seventh-game finish. Heinrich was the batting hero and Joe Page shut down Brooklyn for five innings of sterling relief as the Yankees emerged victorious in game seven. This 1947 Series seemingly opened the door on what was soon to prove a long string of frustrating October losses to the apparently invincible New York Yankees.

In 1948 the heat of racial tensions dulled somewhat on big-league diamonds throughout the land, once Roy Campanella joined Robinson in Brooklyn and Larry Doby played his first full season for Cleveland in the American League, as did ageless veteran Negro League star Satchel Paige. That summer was also a temporary lull in Dodgers fortunes as Boston surged to the top of the senior circuit and St. Louis again sat fast in second. Durocher's men meanwhile tumbled to third, seven and a half games behind the pacesetters. The irrepressible Durocher had returned from his one-year suspension by opening day of 1948, but that incident had brought as its predictable fallout an irrevocable rift between Rickey and his controversial manager. Durocher was out again by mid-season, this time signing on – in a highly improbable move – as the new manager for Brooklyn's long-hated rivals, the crosstown Giants.

By 1949 the full complement of needed players was finally firmly in place for Rickey and his new manager Burt Shotton, and thus the Dodgers charged to their third pennant of the decade. Robinson enjoyed his best career season as league batting

Above: *Cheering teammates carry Cookie Lavagetto to the Dodgers' clubhouse moments after the Brooklyn pinch hitter broke up Yankee Bill Bevens' attempt at a World Series no-hitter on October 3, 1947. Lavagetto's double scored the winning run in game four.*

Right: *It was the sixth inning of game six of the 1947 Series when Al Gionfriddo gained baseball immortality with this miraculous catch of a drive from Joe DiMaggio's bat.*

champion (.342) and MVP, and a brilliant relief outing by Jack Banta during a 10-inning season finale at Philadelphia allowed Brooklyn to hang on this time for a one-game victory over the always contending Cardinals. A rather unspectacular 1949 World Series brought more of the same expected mixture of drama and heart-breaking defeat which was becoming standard fare in head-to-head intra-city combat with the Yankees. This time it was a 4-1 New York advantage, in what was to be the first of five consecutive world titles for the Bronx Bombers under former Daffy Dodger Casey Stengel. This final year of the decade was also the first full season for three stars about to emerge in the decade to come. Duke Snider, Gil Hodges and Don Newcombe all contributed heavily to the Dodgers' pennant chase throughout the summer of 1949, Newcombe winning Rookie-of-the-Year honors, while Snider and Hodges each cracked 23 home runs.

Rickey's Brooklyn Dodgers of the late 1940s will always hold their fascination as baseball's first racially integrated team. It is increasingly difficult – more so with each passing decade – to recapture in print the contemporary impact of Branch Rickey's bold move in signing Robinson. Nor can we

quite appreciate the full daring of young players like Robinson, Bankhead, Campanella, Newcombe and Joe Black, who were the first of their race to tackle a sport exclusively populated by white players throughout three quarters of a century. The Robinson story has been told and retold many times over and the best accounts are perhaps those of journalist Harvey Frommer, historian Julies Tygiel, and Dodgers broadcaster Red Barber, who value accuracy over melodrama.

Yet books can never do complete justice to the fevered tensions disrupting that first integrated baseball season of 1947. Robinson's rookie summer was witness to an outpouring of racial hatred and endless incidents of bigotry and harassment, both on the field of play and within the grandstands and hotels around the league. Rickey's own former team, the Cardinals, threatened to strike rather than play against blacks. St. Louis only took to the field at Brooklyn once league president Frick vowed to suspend the charter of any such uncooperative franchise. An early-season contest at Ebbets Field with Philadelphia brought merciless racial taunts from the Phillies' bench and from manager Ben Chapman. Even Robinson's teammates were less than accepting

In this May 18, 1949 pose, Jackie Robinson (left) and Roy Campanella (right) welcome the young Don Newcombe as he first joins the Dodgers' pitching staff in old Wrigley Field. Newcombe has just reported from the Dodgers' top farm team at Montreal, and will compile a 17-8 record to gain league Rookie of the Year honors while leading Brooklyn to their second league flag in three seasons.

Right: *Unflappable and unassuming Burt Shotton replaced the suspended Durocher at the outset of the 1947 season, and remained the silent binding force behind the Brooklyn team during Jackie Robinson's first tension-filled big-league year. This photo was taken during a game on August 16 as the Dodgers maintained a solid five-game lead over the second-place Cardinals, and pennant hopes looked bright. Shotton, like Connie Mack, did not wear a team uniform – permitted by league rules at the time – and thus had to restrict his managerial presence to the Brooklyn clubhouse and dugout.*

Opposite: *This is the first close-up action photo taken of Jackie Robinson in a big-league game during the historic 1947 season, when Robinson broke baseball's long-standing color barrier. During a final pre-season tune-up game, Robinson is tagged out at third by New York Yankee infielder Bill Johnson, while trying to advance all the way from first on a long single by Pete Reiser.*

at first. Southerner Dixie Walker demanded to be traded rather than play alongside the first black, and Reese and Hodges were reportedly the only Dodgers who struck up genuine clubhouse friendships with Robinson during that first dramatic season.

Rickey's dream of integrating baseball was one that had festered for years before actually being translated into history-making actions. Rickey's biographers have often delighted in recounting the apocryphal incident which reputedly took place while he coached the Ohio Wesleyan college team in 1904, an event which supposedly lit the first fires for racial justice that burned within this religious man. A black first baseman on Rickey's club had been refused a lodging by a South Bend hotel on the eve of Wesleyan's contest against Notre Dame. Upon taking the distraught youngster into his own room, Rickey was deeply touched as he watched the stricken Charlie Thomas weep in agony over the color of his own skin. Mr. Rickey's humanitarian sensitivities likely had as much to do with his integration plans as did his conviction that black talent would provide the winning baseball Brooklyn fans so desperately coveted. Covertly announcing that he was

scouting talent for a negro ball club to play games at Ebbets Field under Dodgers sponsorship, Rickey as early as 1943 put into motion his plan to recruit black talent, assured privately by Commissioner Chandler that the plan would be fully backed by the league's highest office. It was one of Rickey's supreme judgements of human nature and baseball talent, however, that isolated Robinson as the first man to carry the torch of his race in a Brooklyn Dodgers uniform.

What Rickey needed to bring his plan to fruition was a perfect man, one driven with competitive spirit and yet patient enough to take on the full burden of hatred that was to be the inevitable lot of baseball's first black pioneer. Ironically, Robinson may not have been Rickey's man after all, had history conspired a bit differently. A young Cuban infielder named Silvo Garcia had caught Branch Rickey's attention by 1943, and the Mahatma that winter dispatched his personal representative Walter O'Malley to Havana with a letter of credit for $25,000 and instructions to sign Garcia at all costs. Destiny had a script of its own to follow, however, and O'Malley arrived in Cuba only to find that the black star had been recently drafted into the Cuban army and was no longer available for civil employment. Garcia, who might well have been immortalized as the first black big leaguer of the modern era had O'Malley arrived in Cuba a scant week earlier, was later to play out his brief career in relative obscurity as an unheralded star for the New York Cubans of the Negro Professional League.

But Jackie Robinson alone among the many candidates examined by Rickey had the special makeup which the Old Mahatma sought for so important a mission. Robinson's rookie season was full of trials under which any lesser man might well have crumbled – opposing players slashed at him with their spikes, rival benches hurled racial epithets and obscenities, the mail brought death threats and endless harassment from fans across the nation. Yet by the 1949 season Jackie Robinson was a full-blown star and his late career start (he broke in at age 28) was never enough to prevent certain Hall of Fame credentials. Above all else, Jackie Robinson was an endless inspiration to his teammates, with his burning ambition and reckless style of play. Not since Ty Cobb had the American baseball diamond witnessed such fierce – even ruthless – competitive spirit. Paced by Jackie Robinson and loaded with young and talented ballplayers, the Dodgers of Brooklyn were finally on the verge of baseball greatness.

3. Remembering the Glorious Boys of Summer

The "Boys of Summer" pose in the Ebbets Field dugout on July 4, 1951. Pictured are (from left) Jackie Robinson, Don Newcombe, Preacher Roe, Roy Campanella, Pee Wee Reese, Gil Hodges and Duke Snider. If the New York Yankees have long stood out for fans as reviled villains of our loved national pastime, these Dodgers have held our hearts for three generations as the epitome of Brooklyn baseball.

The Dodgers occupying Ebbets Field from the end of World War II until the dawn of West Coast baseball in 1958 are perhaps the most famous and nostalgia-laden team in all baseball history. Author Roger Kahn's best-selling classic, *The Boys of Summer*, has provided this team with its lasting niche and permanent identity for the nation's literate baseball fans. *The Boys of Summer* memorably portrays a dozen teammates from the 1953-1956 Dodgers. These were men who bravely faced the collective pain of diamond defeats throughout their brief baseball careers. They were also men who gallantly struggled with life's larger tragedies once baseball glory was only a proud memory. It was, of course, one of baseball's true ironies – in a sport which derives its very lifeblood from the unexpected moment and the ironic circumstance – that the New York Yankees of Stengel and Mantle and Yogi Berra won World Series upon World Series throughout the 1950s, yet remained for most fans the universally hated symbol of cold, corporate

efficiency. Yet these Dodgers of Campanella and Hodges and Reese – who suffered heart-breaking defeat upon gut-wrenching, late-season calamity – still somehow managed to win lasting devotion from a generation of the nation's baseball fans.

Kahn's book strikes such a nerve among legions of modern baseball fans precisely because the game of baseball is at bottom such a game of bitter and repeated defeats. Seasons, careers, opportunities at baseball immortality are more often lost than won. The Mets of the hapless Polo Ground years or the Cubs of the past three decades are inherently more loveable than the Bronx Bombers of the 1950s or Baltimore's Orioles of the 1970s, simply because they face annual and inevitable defeat with the same stoic resignation as the rest of us. In this respect beyond all others does baseball reflect life – the seemingly endless string of daily disappointments balanced by the unbounded joys of occasional triumph.

The Dodgers of the 1950s were just such a common man's team. For all their prowess,

During the 1952 Series' game six, Edwin "Duke" Snider and Yankee catcher Yogi Berra watch the flight of Snider's eighth-inning homer. Despite his two homers in this game, the Yankees came out on top, 3-2. Snider clubbed over 40 round-trippers in five consecutive seasons (1953-1957), amassing 407 homers in 18 seasons, and compiled 2116 career hits with a lifetime .295 BA.

all their National League pennants and October near-glories, this was a team fated by history to be branded as hopeless losers. In October, when the World Series rolled around, it was always the Bronx Bombers of Gotham who somehow prevailed; it was the Yankees who appeared in every Series between 1949 and 1962 but two, winning an unprecedented five World Titles in succession. This Dodgers team might have been the second best team in baseball, but it was only the second best team in the City of New York!

But history and time have conspired to blur the picture of the Dodgers franchise in the final years of Branch Rickey and the initial years of Walter O'Malley. Kahn and other writers have sentimentalized the tough defeats and sudden calamities, but baseball historians John Bowman and Joel Zoss suggest a far different picture – one more in line with the hard facts of baseball's statistical realities. This was one of the National League's best teams ever, a team so dominating in their own league for over a decade that their achievements fall only a whisker below those of the vaunted American League Yankees themselves.

Between 1946 and 1956 there were six pennants won at Ebbets Field, with three more barely lost by the narrowest of margins. A five-game deficit to the Giants during the second-place finish of 1954 represents the only season in this entire stretch of marvelous summers where a pennant was neither won nor lost on the season's final day. A third-place 1948 campaign (seven and a half games behind Boston) represents the only summer in 11 that the Dodgers were not serious contenders until the season's final week. Vic-

tories on the final day of the campaign in 1946, 1950 and 1951 would, in fact, have given Brooklyn an unprecedented nine of eleven pennants, and only 19 more victories (less than two a year!) between 1946 and 1956 would have resulted in an unimaginable 11 consecutive National League flags! Even the Yankees never accomplished that kind of league domination.

Also this was one of the most colorful, star-studded teams in the history of National League baseball. Duke Snider, Roy Campanella, Gil Hodges, Pee Wee Reese, Jackie Robinson, Carl Furillo, Don Newcombe, Carl Erskine, Preacher Roe, Sal Maglie – the lineup reads like an all-time Dodgers roster for the decades rather than a daily batting order to be sent out to battle each day for most of a decade. The lineup included four Hall of Famers, four additional perennial All-Stars, and some of the best defensive stars in the game as well in third baseman Billy Cox, second sacker Junior Gilliam, and shotgun right fielder Carl Furillo.

Offense was of course the Dodgers' strongest suit. The slugging trio of Snider, Campanella and Hodges enjoyed five consecutive seasons during which they hit an aggregate 100 or more home runs; Reese and Robinson were base-stealers without parallel in an era which unfortunately placed altogether too little emphasis on aggressive base-running; Dodger hitters accounted for two batting titles (Robinson in 1949; Furillo in 1953), one home run crown (Snider in 1956), two RBI standards (Campanella in 1953; Snider in 1955), and four stolen base champions (Reiser in 1946; Robinson in 1947 and 1949; Reese in 1952) during the 1946-1956 era. Pitching and

Salvatore "The Barber" Maglie hurled for 10 years in the bigs, plus a stint in the outlawed Mexican League during the 1940s as well. Sporting a phenomenal lifetime record of 119-62 (3.15 ERA), Maglie was first a Dodger nemesis when with the Giants in 1950-55, then later a mainstay of the Brooklyn staff in 1956-57. Maglie's liberal use of the chin-tight knockdown pitch earned his colorful nickname.

nella, Hodges, Robinson and Reese were regulars at their positions between 1949 and 1953. Newcombe pitched in each of the 1949-1951 mid-summer classics, and again in 1955, while Ralph Branca and Clem Labine also made All-Star Game appearances during this decade. Durocher managed the 1948 National League All-Stars; Burt Shotton was the 1950 pilot; Charlie Dressen directed the Senior Circuit from the bench in 1953; and Walter Alston managed for the National League in 1954, 1956 and 1957. In all, an aggregate total of 62 Dodgers appeared on All-Star Game rosters between 1947 and 1957, with Reese (eight appearances), Snider (seven appearances), and Campanella (also seven appearances) leading the way. Again only the Yankees of the same era could boast such a lineup of league All-Stars across all nine diamond positions.

Finally, this team enjoyed as well a unique relationship with the sprawling yet close-knit community that supported it. The Dodgers of the 1940s and 1950s were a big-city team with a distinctly small-town identity. The borough of Brooklyn, it seems, took its identity to an extraordinary degree from the local ballpark and the big-league ballplayers for which it was home. With the unmatchable aid of hindsight, some historians now view this phenomenon of the Dodgers during the Jackie Robinson era to be largely a myth of convenience, however – a product of half-truth and exaggeration born from a generation of expatriate Brooklynites longing to recapture the roots of community. Cultural anthropologist Frederic Roberts, for one, argues that this Dodgers myth – of a huge homogeneous borough unanimously united behind its loveable ball team "that dwelled at the center of its universe" – has little basis in historical fact. Roberts suggests that it is largely a perverse 1970s-1980s reflection of "the role of sports as a common language for communicating about American experience" and has thus been "a way for Brooklyn refugees (many of them intellectuals and most Jewish) to connect with new environments while retaining a sense of loyalty to the home borough." Roberts acknowledges, of course, the hundreds of popular culture references (in plays, novels, TV shows, and literature of all types) which intimately link Brooklyn and Brooklynites with the favored home team as symbol of Brooklyn's unmatched community pride. In an age before television, Brooklyn fans came to the ballpark with regularity and thus knew their local heroes intimately. If the present-day legends surrounding the passionate following of the hometown Dodgers during the

defense did not lag very far behind, though some would contend that it was a shortage of dominant pitching that was always the Dodger nemesis in late-season pennant drives and World Series play. Don Newcombe did win over 17 games on five separate occasions, and the relief pitching of Labine, Maglie, Loes and Bessent was perhaps the best of the era in the senior circuit. Only starting pitching seemed a sustained weakness, with steady Carl Erskine (11 or more victories for six consecutive seasons) the single reliable starter year-in and year-out behind the tireless Newcombe.

One measure of the dominance of this team that Rickey had assembled in the late 1940s and O'Malley sustained throughout most of the 1950s was the endless parade of National League All-Stars – both starters and reserves – throughout the first decade to follow World War II. Snider, Campa-

1950s is indeed largely the stuff of popular myth, then like all myths this one seems to have sustained a life of its own.

Still if it is true that every Brooklynite of the early 1950s was not a passionate Dodgers fan – or even a baseball fan – those who were witnessed some of the most exciting baseball of the modern era. The 1950 National League flag was ultimately captured on the season's final day by an upstart Philadelphia Phillies team that has been known to the ages as simply "the Whiz Kids." In a single-season burst of glory, a young Philadelphia team (the average age of such stars as Richie Ashburn, Dick Sisler, ace hurlers Curt Simmons and Robin Roberts, and MVP fireballer Jim Konstanty, was a mere 26) hung on until season's end to capture their first title in 35 long seasons. Robin Roberts paced a strong Philadelphia staff with 20 victories and Konstanty become the first relief pitcher ever to gain MVP honors.

But the Phillies' glorious pennant year did not come easy, and late season Dodgers heroics almost saved the day for rabid Ebbets Field rooters. Holding a seven-game margin over the Dodgers with but 11 contests remaining, the Phils of manager Eddie Sawyer saw their vaunted pitching staff decimated by injury at season's end, and their pennant dreams reduced to a final season's game against Brooklyn on October 1st. That final crucial Ebbets Field contest was not only one of the most ill-fated and memorable of Dodgers history, but perhaps ranks second only to the 1951 Polo Grounds finale in the annals of historic National League pennant contests. Newcombe and Roberts battled 1-1 until the ninth, when the Dodgers opened their last at-bat with men at first and second and none out. The Dodgers enjoyed a moment of euphoric hope when Duke Snider singled to center, but Richie Ashburn scooped up Snider's liner and gunned down Dodgers runner Cal Abrams at the plate. This set the stage for a dramatic tenth inning in which journeyman outfielder Dick Sisler (son of Hall of Famer George Sisler) smashed a three-run homer to end the valiant Dodgers' late surge.

The 1950 season had brought with it, however, numerous signs of the bright Dodgers future which lay ahead. In late August Gil Hodges belted four homers in a single Ebbets Field game – a 19-3 pasting of the Boston Braves – to become only the fourth National Leaguer and sixth big leaguer to accomplish such a slugging feat. Snider lead the senior circuit in total bases, and Brooklyn as a team paced the league by a wide margin in both batting and slugging averages. Jackie Robinson (.328 BA) en-

joyed one of his finest seasons in 1950 as well, finishing second to Stan Musial (.346 BA) for the league batting crown, while teammate Snider (.321) followed in third position among the league's best hitters.

With the arrival of spring training at Vero Beach, Florida, in 1951, it looked at long last to the faithful in Flatbush that the much anticipated "next year" had finally indeed arrived. This seemed destined to be the season in which the Bums would at long last shed their well-worn image as annual losers; the Phillies seemed an overnight flash, devastated in the 1950 World Series by the proud Yankees, and Brooklyn again returned a lineup that was arguably the strongest in either league. The season itself, spiced with the sudden return to prominence by the Giants of Leo Durocher and the exciting rookie play of electrifying Willie Mays, was again a close race that

Pee Wee Reese takes a toss from Gil Hodges to force the sliding Billy Martin during 1955 World Series game action at Yankee Stadium. The Yankees won this sixth Series game, 5-1, forcing the historic game seven encounter that led to a first and only Brooklyn World Championship victory over those hated rivals from the nearby Bronx.

stretched till the final days of September. Sparked by the arrival of Mays in late May, New York roared down the stretch in August of 1951 with the most torrid finish since the "Miracle Braves" of 1914. Winning 16 straight between August 12th and September 9th (while the Dodgers were playing .500 ball over the same stretch), Durocher's men then won 16 of their final

20 to close a five-and-a-half game Dodgers lead and force the National League's second-ever post-season playoff series. It was only Jackie Robinson's own heroics on the final afternoon in Philadelphia that had prevented New York from sweeping past the Dodgers at regular season's end. Repaying the Phils for the finale of 1950, Robinson saved the Dodgers with a miraculous catch of an Eddie Waitkus liner in the 12th with the bases loaded; he then proceeded to produce the game-winner, with perhaps the Dodgers' most dramatic home run ever, in the top of the 14th. The 1951 season was truly destined to end with a thunderous bang – two of the most dramatic moments in all Dodgers history – one of them euphoric, the other lined with the darkest tragedy.

Events of the final Dodgers-Giants playoff game of October 1951 have been told over and over again down through the years. The "Miracle at Coogan's Bluff" – as it is now known – is perhaps the most widely discussed single moment of baseball's history. It is estimated that three million or more family television sets were tuned to the National League Championship game that day, and Bobby Thomson's dramatic game-ending, ninth-inning homer was perhaps the nation's first major sporting moment viewed simultaneously by a live national audience. For generations of fans the vivid image has remained of Thomson rounding third and heading for

Right: *Preacher Roe, left-handed ace of the Dodgers' staff between 1948 and 1954, won 93 and lost only 37 for Brooklyn. Admitting openly that he threw the illegal spitter, which along with crafty changes of speed made him one of the toughest NL hurlers of the 1950s, Roe twice led the circuit in winning percentage (.714 in 1949 and .888 – at 22-3 – in 1951). Owning one of the best lifetime percentage marks (.627), Roe hung up his glove in 1954, just one season before Brooklyn at last won it all.*

Right: *We did it! Jubilant Dodgers surround manager Chuck Dressen as they whoop it up after whipping the Philadelphia Phillies in the first game of a doubleheader at Ebbets Field. The date was September 23, 1952, and Brooklyn had just won the NL crown to rebound from that crushing defeat at season's end in 1951. Around the corner was still another futile rematch in the Fall Classic with the AL Champion Yankees.*

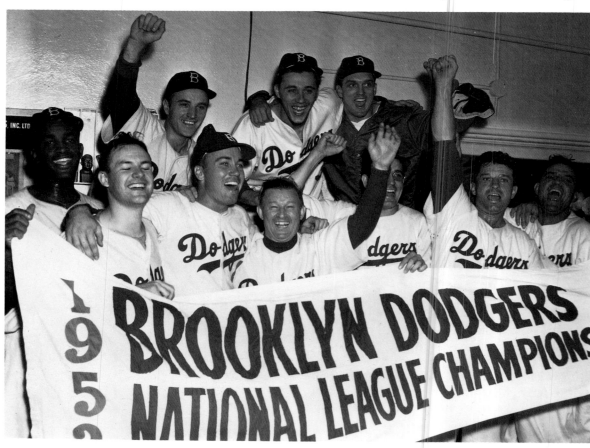

a mob of waiting teammates at the plate, manager Durocher leaping in hot pursuit from the third base coaching box, the dejected Dodgers hurler (with the ominous number 13 in full view on his uniform back) strolling forlornly to the distant Brooklyn clubhouse in deep center field. The 1951 Dodgers seemed an invincible team at the outset. Hodges hit 40 homers that year; Robinson batted .338; Preacher Roe compiled an incredible 22-3 mark on the hill; the Brooklyn juggernaut paced the league in almost all offensive categories: homers, RBIs, hits, doubles, stolen bases, batting average, slugging percentage and even double plays. But it was not enough as Thomson's timely three-run homer brought a pennant-clinching 5-4 victory for the Giants and an improbable last-minute triumph in the rare, best-of-three, tie-breaking, overtime series. Again the frustrated Brooklyns would have to hope helplessly for the promise of another "next year." One must contemplate the deep ironies of the famous Sisler and Thomson pennant-winning homers of 1950 and 1951. If these brief moments of baseball history could be somehow reversed, Brooklyn would have matched the rival Yankees of the 1949-1953 period virtually step-for-step. Like the Bronx Bombers, Brooklyn would also have appeared in five consecutive World Series match-ups, taking five National League crowns in a row. If the Dodgers and Yankees so dominated baseball of the early 1950s in their rival leagues, think what might have transpired had only Sisler and Thomson failed to wrench two pennants from Brooklyn's grasp. Yet again, perhaps it was these very defeats that made the Dodgers the nearly unbeatable club they were to become between 1952 and 1956. For Brooklyn was to arise from the ashes of Coogan's Bluff to return stronger and more determined than ever for the subsequent half-dozen National League campaigns.

The pennant races of 1952 and 1953 were never much in doubt as the strengthened Brooklyn team glided home four and a half games ahead of the Giants in 1952, and then raced to a 13-game advantage over the upstart, transplanted Milwaukee Braves in 1953. The Giants had threatened to rival the Dodgers again in 1952, but the early-season loss of sophomore sensation Willie Mays to Army induction in May ended any serious hopes for another "Miracle at Coogan's Bluff," and left New York in strong but hopeless pursuit of powerful Brooklyn. The Dodgers' own loss of ace Don Newcombe to the military was largely offset by the sensational rookie season of pitcher Joe Black (15-4, 15 saves, 2.15 ERA). Although

taking Rookie-of-the-Year honors, Black ironically did not post sufficient innings pitched however to earn the league's ERA crown, that title going to another outstanding rookie, future Hall of Famer Hoyt Wilhelm of the Giants (2.43).

Much of the story of the 1953 campaign was the Braves – newly settled in Milwaukee as a result of the first major-league franchise shift of the century, and compiling a subsequent National League home attendance mark of 1,826,397. Yet the on-field play of the Braves was no match for the powerful Dodgers; paced by Erskine's pitching (20-6) and the league-leading .344 BA of Carl Furillo, Brooklyn amassed 105 victories under third-year manager Charlie Dressen, the most in franchise history. The Braves and Dodgers teams of 1953 were perhaps the two most potent lineups ever to take the field in the same National League season. Milwaukee boasted the league's best pitching staff, paced by veteran Warren Spahn who lead the league in both victories (23-7) and ERA (2.10), and the powerful hitting of third sacker Eddie Mathews, tops in the league in homers (47) and second in RBIs (135). But Brooklyn had even more hitting, with five regulars (Furillo, Hodges, Snider, Robinson, Campanella) batting over .300, Snider and Campanella both surpassing 40 homers, and Campanella leading in RBIs (142) and achieving the coveted league MVP Award for the second time in three seasons. To add to the luster of this most powerful of all Dodgers teams, second base-

The young rookie outfielder Carl Furillo poses in his patented outfield stance near the close of the 1946 season. Furillo was an unsung hero of the "Boys of Summer" era team, once leading the NL in batting (.344 in 1953), and compiling a 15-year lifetime BA of .299 while smacking 192 career homers. But Furillo will best be remembered for one of the greatest throwing arms ever possessed by a big-league outfielder, as well as his uncanny ability to play caroms off the difficult sloped right-field wall of Ebbets Field.

A three-frame sequence captures Carl Erskine showing the no-hit form he displayed on June 19, 1952, while hurling the first of two career masterpieces. This one was a 5-0 victory over the Chicago Cubs in Ebbets Field, which earned a substantial $500 bonus check from Walter O'Malley. Erskine draws a bead (left) on a strike target and cranks his deadly throwing arm, draws back to let fly (center), then unleashes the pitch (right) to the game's last enemy batter Eddie Miksis. A single base on balls stood as the lone blemish on Erskine's near perfect effort.

man Jim Gilliam won Rookie-of-the-Year honors and the Brooklyn team batting average (.285) was a full 20 points better than that of the second-place Braves.

World Series play in both 1952 and 1953 seemed near carbon copies of the 1947 and 1949 Dodgers-Yankees subway series. The 1952 Series is perhaps best remembered for the failures of slugging first baseman Gil Hodges who, despite 32 homers and 102 RBIs in regular season play, could not muster a single hit in 21 Series at-bats. While the Dodgers won the first, third and fifth games, including two of the three games played in Yankee Stadium, the Yankees roared back with two final victories at Ebbets Field, sending the ill-fated Dodgers to their sixth consecutive World Series defeat. The 1953 Series saw more of the same, this time a four-games-to-two margin for the Bronx Bombers, despite the rebound of Hodges, with a .364 average, and a Brooklyn team batting average of .300 for the Series. The true highlight of the 1953 Series, however – the Dodgers' seventh consecutive without victory – was Erskine's record 14 strikeouts (four against Mantle) in game three, a 3-2 Dodgers win in Ebbets Field. Erskine's masterpiece game, along with his first no-hitter against the Cubs in June of 1952, had established the Indiana right-hander by season's end as the new ace of a Brooklyn staff weakened by Newcombe's military tour, and apparently an insufficient match for the Yankees' awesome starting rotation of Allie Reynolds, Vic Raschi, Eddie Lopat, and Whitey Ford.

The 1954 campaign was something of a surprise off-year in Brooklyn, as the Giants again rebounded under the inspired play of Willie Mays and the managerial skills of ex-Dodger skipper Durocher. Fresh from military service, Mays batted a league-leading .345 and stroked 41 homers. Not that the Dodgers played badly, but 92 victories were not enough to make for a close pennant race throughout most of the summer of 1954. Erskine again won 18, but the newly returned Don Newcombe was off form (9-8, 4.55 ERA), and the Dodgers limped home second, five games out. But all this was only a quiet prelude for the long-awaited heroics and considerable fireworks of the 1955 campaign, for 1954 had brought an important change to the Dodgers franchise, one that was to pay incalculable dividends for the course of the next two decades. When skipper Charlie Dressen had demanded a long-term contract after the 1953 World Series loss, Walter O'Malley wasted little time in dispatching Dressen and replacing him with a little-known organization man, Walter Emmons Alston, a failed player with only one big-league at-bat, yet a successful minor-league manager long groomed by Branch Rickey as the future big-league skipper of the Dodgers. Alston's soft-spoken ways and hands-off clubhouse policies were, as it turned out, the final catalyst necessary to turn these power-hitting Dodgers into the unbeatable champions that Brooklyn faithful had long expected to emerge.

There was little serious challenge for the

1955 edition of the Dodgers, the second under Alston, as they pulled away early with 22 victories in their first 24 games, building a nine-and-a-half game lead by the end of April and never looking back at the trailing Braves (13 and a half games) and Giants (18 and a half games). Again a Dodgers-Yankees Series was the familiar venue for the fall of 1955. Yet this was fated to be a year in which it would all be somehow different. Just when it seemed like the Dodgers would never manage to win the big games in October, baseball fate smiled fondly on the long-suffering Dodger fans and intervened in the form of some much-needed pitching help. Don Newcombe had returned to earlier form with a 20-5 1955 record, and durable Clem Labine had led the senior circuit that season with 60 game appearances. Yet it was a young, third-year pitcher with a lifetime 29-21 mark who unexpectedly emerged as the most robust of all Dodgers World Series heroes. Under the spectacular hurling of lefty Johnny Podres (Series 2-0, 1.00 ERA), the Dodgers finally were to shut down the powerful Yankees and accomplish what no Brooklyn team ever had before.

When the dust settled on 1955 World Series play, the Dodgers had finally emerged with a 4-3 Series triumph, keyed by Podres' brilliant seventh-game shutout pitching, Hodges' two RBIs in that final, dramatic, 2-0 game, and the memorable defensive gem of journeyman outfielder Sandy Amoros in the sixth inning of that most treasured game in Dodgers baseball history. With two men aboard and Berra at bat, Amoros had raced deep to the left-field corner to rob Berra of a certain hit and the game-tying RBIs. Finally the bridesmaids were bridesmaids no more, and the entire borough of Brooklyn was overcome with celebration of its first and only baseball World Championship. It was Podres' brilliant pitching on October 4th of 1955 that was most responsible for the championship season of 1955, yet Snider's four homers and .320 BA, as well as timely relief pitching by Clem Labine in game four (in which he earned the victory) and game five (in which he was credited with the save) played significant roles as well.

The summer of 1956 brought new challenges to the first Dodgers team ever to defend a World Title in Ebbets Field. A torrid summer found the Dodgers nipping out Milwaukee by one game and the power-laden Cincinnati team by a mere two, in one of the tightest pennant races of the decade. The old order was now finally passing away and new faces were appearing all too slowly to plug the increasing gaps in manager Alston's veteran team. The 1956 season would be Jackie Robinson's last; Billy Cox was gone as a fixture in the infield; as was Preacher Roe from the mound. Joe Black had faded as rapidly as he had appeared, and was toiling again in the minors by 1954 before being traded to Cincinnati in 1955. But the Dodgers' lineup that Alston fielded in 1956 was still awesome and experienced, and another pennant was the inevitable result. It didn't seem easy this time around, though, and the Dodgers needed a final-day victory over the Pirates – Don Newcombe's 27th win of the campaign – to assure a pennant victory. Newcombe, enjoying the finest season of his career, was appropriately honored for his effort with the first-ever Cy Young Award.

The 1956 World Series was perhaps the most anticlimactic in Dodgers history — another tight, seven-game Series lost in almost predictable fashion to the crosstown, rival Yankees. Yet this was a Series always to be remembered for a single, dramatic game. As had happened with Podres and Amoros the season before, or with Bill

Below: *Etched in the minds of Dodger fans everywhere is the strong-arm lefty form of Yankee-killer Johnny Podres as he shut down the Bronx Bombers 2-0 in the finale of the 1955 World Series and brought Brooklyn its first and only world title. This action is from June of that same season, a campaign in which Podres posted a mediocre 9-10 won-lost mark. The little lefty from Witherbee, New York, would enjoy five consecutive winning seasons in LA (1959-63), and posted a sterling 18-5 mark in 1961.*

Like Jackie Robinson, Roy Campanella was a true pioneer in the racial integration of baseball, yet a less flashy player and less forceful personality, who had always moved in Robinson's gigantic shadow. It was a position which the quiet Campy never begrudged, and perhaps even relished. While Robinson burned with a smoldering fire, Campanella exuded good humor off the field and spoke baseball thunder with his reckless bat alone. In a career no longer than Robinson's, and cut off in its prime by a tragic automobile wreck, Campy bashed 242 career homers (third on the all-time Dodgers list), established a Brooklyn single-season RBI standard in 1953 with 142, and earned three NL MVP selections (1951, 1953, 1955).

Bevens and Cookie Lavagetto in 1947, World Series play often selects the most unlikely heroes to capture the nation's imagination for one brief day of immeasurable glory. On October 8th of 1956, in Series game five, Yankee Don Larsen achieved baseball immortality with the first and only no-hitter (a perfect game at that) in the annals of the nation's Fall Classic. Lar- sen's perfect game was almost the singular career highlight of a pitcher who was to win 81 big-league games, yet lose 91, while pitching with eight different teams over 14 mediocre seasons. Larsen's single day of glory also provided the death knell for another frustrating Dodgers summer in aging Ebbets Field, as the Yankees took the second of the final two games at Ebbets

Field to register their sixth Series title in seven tries against Brooklyn. While few could perhaps sense it at the time, that final Series game of October 10, 1956, was also the last ever to be played by a team wearing the Brooklyn uniform.

The year 1957 was destined to be the final season in Brooklyn, though not everyone realized this when the Dodgers broke spring training camp in Vero Beach that April. The signs of impending divorce between Walter O'Malley and the community which had so long sustained the Dodgers' rich baseball tradition were already in the air, of course. Brooklyn had scheduled seven "home games" in Jersey City Stadium in 1956 – one against each other National League rival – and again in 1957. O'Malley chafed under the knowledge that Milwaukee's Braves, with their new showcase stadium, continued to draw over two million spectators each season between

1954 and 1957. The 1957 baseball season itself was downbeat and quiet for Brooklyn. The ever-improving Braves won 95 ball games and finished eight lengths in front of the second-place Cardinals, and 11 full games above the fading Dodgers, who limped home 14 games over .500. While Snider hit 40 homers again and Furillo batted a little over .300, for the first time in almost a decade the Dodgers failed to lead the National League in a single offensive category. This was an altogether anticlimactic and unfitting end for the glorious tradition of Dodger baseball in the borough of Brooklyn, which had provided so many thrills and heroes during the glorious dozen seasons that had followed World War II. Yet as the end came for Brooklyn baseball, most fans – for all the obvious signs of the previous two seasons – still didn't realize that the demise of their beloved team was quite so near at hand.

Carl Erskine, slated to pitch the April 13, 1954 season's opener against the rival New York Giants, here confers with new Brooklyn manager Walter Alston during a practice session at Ebbets Field the day before. Erskine was just coming off his best career year, having won 20 and posted a league-leading .769 winning percentage. Alston, of course, was about to enjoy the first of his 23 seasons at the helm for O'Malley.

4. New Beginnings— O'Malley's Dodgers Move West

Walter O'Malley had risen slowly and unobtrusively within the Dodgers organization under Branch Rickey, serving first as trusted financial lawyer chosen to represent the Brooklyn Trust Company's interests in the club, later as Mr. Rickey's general assistant, handy advisor, occasional scout and emissary, and all-purpose right-hand man. It was O'Malley that Mr. Rickey had sent winging to Havana in late 1944 on an unsuccessful mission to recruit Black Cuban star Silvio Garcia. But O'Malley himself had originally arrived on the scene little more than a year earlier, when heirs of Ed McKeever finally sold their quarter-interest in the franchise to a makeshift triumvirate of local investors. This group was organized by Brooklyn Trust President George McLaughlin, and consisted of Rickey, John L. Smith of the Pfizer Chemical Company, and Walter O'Malley as McLaughlin's own personal representative. Thus O'Malley's first inroads with the team ironically came in the very deal which was also to spell the inevitable downfall of the old Mahatma himself, though few (except perhaps McLaughlin) could see any of this at the time.

By 1944 the new ruling troika had pur-

chased as well the remaining 50-percent share in the club still controlled by the heirs of Charles Ebbets, cementing their firm grip on ownership of the Dodger franchise. While Branch Rickey seemed in full control of Dodgers baseball operations throughout the final years of the 1940s, Walter O'Malley's front-office power grew exponentially as well, and the two giants hurtled silently toward a cataclysmic financial showdown that would come about late in the season of 1950.

Against this backdrop of financial restructuring there was played out also the fascinating personal relationship between Rickey and his volatile field manager Leo Durocher. The two could not have been more different in personality and temperament – Rickey the very image of quiet piety and Durocher the figure of fast friends, fast lifestyle and fast tongue. Yet Rickey long held abiding respect for Durocher and his abilities, and had often intervened to smooth the way for Leo in his turbulent years under Frankie Frisch at St. Louis. Like Larry MacPhail before him, the Dodgers' president and general manager held a world of respect for Durocher's brashness and mental toughness, while at

Members of the Dodger brain trust have gathered in the club offices on December 5, 1947, presumably to discuss who will be the Dodgers' manager for 1948. The seemingly jovial group includes (from left) coach Ray Blades, coach Clyde Sukeforth, manager Burt Shotton, president Branch Rickey, and coach Jake Pitler. Player assignments for the entire farm system can be seen in the background.

the same time deploring his widely publicized off-field antics, as well as his often turbulent on-field behavior. The highly religious Rickey seemed to see in the incorrigible Durocher his pet reclamation project, and was tolerant of his manager's frequent battles with umpires and occasional sanctions from league president Ford Frick. Much of Rickey's aloofness from Durocher's constant brushes with the law (he was once arrested for battering a fan, and the club had to settle a civil suit out of court for $6,500) may well have had to do with the Mahatma's own preoccupations in the early 1940s with launching his noble baseball integration experiment. The promise and plight of Jackie Robinson was apparently much more on the Mahatma's mind than the antics of his fiery manager. Ironically, when Robinson took the field for his rookie season in 1947, Durocher was not around for the action, being sentenced that very season to serve out his one-year suspension for ill-advised associations with known gamblers.

Durocher's chaotic reign as Dodgers manager was punctuated with brief appearances by another important figure in Brooklyn baseball history of the 1940s – Branch Rickey's long-time friend, Burton (Barney) Shotton. While his own role has been somewhat diminished by the passage of time, Burt Shotton was a significant figure in Dodgers baseball at the end of the Rickey era. When Rickey called upon the 63-year-old Shotton to come out of retirement in Florida a week into the 1947 season and take over for the suspended Durocher, no managerial position in baseball could have been more pressure-packed and explosive. Jackie Robinson had just been introduced to the league and tension was as high among Robinson's own Dodger teammates as it was throughout the remainder of the league. Shotton, who had managed the Phillies and Reds for seven seasons in the 1930s, had been away from the National League since 1934 when he graciously answered the call of his old friend in 1947; he admirably handled the job that had been turned down by both Dodger coach Clyde Sukeforth and ex-Yankee skipper Joe McCarthy, and rewarded Rickey's faith with a reunified Brooklyn team and a league title during that historic 1947 season. When Durocher's return to the Brooklyn bench lasted less than a full season in 1948, it was again Burt Shotton who answered Rickey's call shortly after the All-Star break to return to the dugout at Ebbets Field. While he was able to salvage little of the 1948 campaign, Shotton again led the Dodgers to the World Series in 1949, as well as to the thrilling if heartbreaking

second-place finish behind Philadelphia during 1950. Manager Shotton was a most unimposing figure in Brooklyn, a stark contrast to his predecessor Durocher and his successor Charlie Dressen. Adopting the old-style pose of Connie Mack and refusing to wear a team uniform, Shotton remained an unnoticed figure in street clothes sequestered on the Brooklyn bench during game play. The quieting influence and leadership which he brought to the Dodgers' clubhouse during the early Robinson years, however, is a final and enduring monument to one of the most mysterious and underrated figures in the annals of Brooklyn baseball.

O'Malley seized power in 1950 and quickly consolidated his iron-fisted control over the Dodgers' front office and on-field fortunes. When O'Malley, Rickey and John L. Smith had put up $350,000 each to purchase 75 percent of the Brooklyn team stock from the remaining Ebbets and McKeever heirs, Rickey's own limited financial resources had forced the Mahatma into further indebtedness in order to come up with his own share of the pot. Rickey had chafed under this arrangement for several years, and finally informed his partners in 1949 that he was interested in selling off his own stock – for an asking price of $1 million. Rickey skillfully trapped his displeased partners into matching precisely such an extravagant sum; through intervention of his long-time friend John Galbreath – owner of the Pittsburgh Pirates - a prospective buyer for Rickey's share was arranged in New York tycoon William Zeckendorf. Zeckendorf's offer of $1.05 million was reluctantly met by O'Malley and Smith, yet matters were further complicated by Smith's own death and the October 1950 expiration date of Rickey's own contract as

Owner Branch Rickey chats with manager Leo Durocher (left) at a spring training facility in the West Point (New York) Field House, March 1943. Rickey, of course, is the man ultimately responsible for the legend that was to be Jackie Robinson and the heroic figure that was Roy Campanella, as well as for much of the shape and color of the game of baseball as we know it today. A deeply religious man, Rickey shunned ball games on Sundays, a decision that prematurely ended his own first big-league playing opportunity before he even appeared in a single game for Cincinnati in 1904.

Right: Celebrating their World Championship at the Dodgers' victory party in the Hotel Bossert on October 4, 1955, are (from left) World Series hitting star Duke Snider; NL president Warren Giles; club president Walter O'Malley; pitching sensation Johnny Podres, winner of two Series games; and Gil Hodges, who was responsible for batting in the only two Dodger runs in the final game.

Above: Chuck Dressen hopes to be a Giant-killer as he mugs before the initial playoff game between the Dodgers and Giants at Ebbets Field on October 1, 1951. The Giants were to take that first game 3-1 behind Jim Hearn; Clem Labine would pitch Brooklyn to a 10-0 triumph in game two. Only two days after this photo, Bobby Thomson's crushing "shot heard round the world" robbed the Dodgers and Dressen of the cherished NL flag in his rookie season at the Dodger helm.

club general manager. Upon matching Zeckendorf's offer and meeting Rickey's sale price, the angered O'Malley moved quickly to clean house of his antagonistic former partner and his associates. Rickey gracefully announced his resignation at a jam-packed press conference in Brooklyn's Hotel Bossert on October 26, 1950, and Burt Shotton was replaced only weeks later by Charlie Dressen as field pilot. Rickey himself was hired by John Galbreath as the Pirates' general manager and moved into his new position considerably wealthier than he had ever been before. O'Malley, in turn, had been left so angered by Rickey's extraction of such an exorbitant price in payment for control of the Dodgers that he expunged the very memory of the Mahatma from the Dodgers' front office establishment. For years after the departure of Branch Rickey from Brooklyn, there remained an office rule in team headquarters that anyone so much as even mentioning Rickey's name was to be punished with a token fine of one dollar.

Many of Walter O'Malley's strategic moves after he took over control in Brooklyn were to pay rich dividends. Charlie Dressen was a talented baseball man and successful leader who took an increasingly mature Dodgers team to two pennants and one second-place finish in his three years at the helm, and had it not been for Thomson's legendary Polo Grounds homer in 1951 it would have been three successive pennants. When Dressen demanded an end to O'Malley's policy of one-year renewable contracts for the managerial post, his replacement by unknown Rickey protege Walter Alston was to usher in the most successful managerial reign in all of National League history. Young O'Malley staffers Emil (Buzzy) Bavasi and Fresco Thompson became team vice-presidents, the former ascending to general manager of "the big club" and the latter successfully managing the team's extensive farm team operation which consisted of over 20 thriving affiliations.

The baseball talent that was to see the Dodgers through their championship years in the 1950s had, of course, already been put in place by Rickey and, before him, Larry MacPhail. When it came to acquiring and keeping ballplayers, O'Malley did not have the extraordinary talent or good fortune of his two unrivaled predecessors. One disastrous player personnel decision, in particular, made by Dodger executives during the first years under O'Malley, has been almost lost in the luster of Dodger pennants amassed throughout that era. In February of 1954 Dodger brass inked a $15,000 bonus contract with a 20-year-old Puerto Rican outfield prospect who was assigned directly to their top Montreal farm club at the conclusion of training camp that spring. It was the thinking of the Dodgers' brain trust that Roberto Clemente was not yet ready to supplant Snider, Furillo or even journey-man George Shuba in the Ebbets Field pastures. It was also their hope that the talented youngster would be unnoticed in Montreal and thus not spirited away through the league's new bonus draft rule – any player signed for a bonus exceeding $4,000 was subject to irrevocable draft by the opposition if he did not remain on the big-league roster for the entire first season. The Dodgers frustrated the young Clemente by hiding him on the Montreal bench throughout the 1954 summer. Yet Branch Rickey's new team, the Pirates, were as stocked with astute talent scouts as all earlier Rickey organizations, and when the Pirates finished last in 1954, Mr. Rickey had an appropriate moment of revenge against O'Malley and his former employers. When Rickey plucked Clemente – one of baseball's all-time greats – from the Dodger roster in the winter of 1954, he did more than secure the future of the Pittsburgh franchise. Gone forever was the possibility for Brooklyn fans of the mid-1950s of seeing perhaps the greatest outfield ever assembled – Furillo in right, Snider in center, Clemente in right. Gone as well was the havoc Clemente might have wreaked during the following decade, faced with the short left-field porch of the L. A. Coliseum and the cozy quarters of O'Malley's Dodger Stadium.

Walter O'Malley's dream of a new home for the Dodgers actually began sometime in the early 1950s, though it was cleverly hidden from public view, just as Rickey's true ambitions for baseball integration had been carefully masked from public display a decade earlier. O'Malley was long and justifiably frustrated in his modernization plans by New York City officials, as well as by the built-in insufficiencies of aging Ebbets Field itself. He did commission plans for revamping his ancient ballpark, but these proved futile, given the inherent expense of such a plan and the fact that Ebbets Field occupied an entire city block and could not be extended into surrounding thoroughfares. Although several sites for a new park were suggested to city officials on downtown Brooklyn Avenue along Atlantic Avenue, the city refused to act. Thus the ultimate blame for departure of the team from its home of nearly seven decades is to be in part laid upon the obstinacy of the city fathers themselves, as much as it is to be credited to the pure greed of Mr. O'Malley. O'Malley has not been treated at all kindly by recent baseball historians, of course, but his motive in moving the franchise may not have been as entirely unreasonable and self-serving as is commonly portrayed. More objective onlookers now see New York Parks Commissioner and power-broker Robert Moses as equal villain in the

At Spring Training in Vero Beach in early March of 1958, the newly christened Los Angeles Dodgers pose around a banner displaying the name of their new home town. The opening game of West Coast baseball, with San Francisco's Giants in tiny Seals Stadium on April 15, was little more than a month away, as was the home opener at the LA Coliseum on April 18. Labine, Hodges and Snider (above the letters LES) seem preoccupied with their private conversation and seem anything but displaced by the new logo which now adorns their Dodger caps.

drama which spirited the Dodgers away from Brooklyn.

O'Malley went about his planned West Coast move with considerable guile and efficiency. First came the selling of the land on which Ebbets Field stood to a New York real estate developer who planned an apartment complex once the Dodgers obtained their new park. Next was a clever deal to obtain rights to the Los Angeles minor-league franchise and its stadium as well. O'Malley conspired with Philip Wrigley to exchange the Dodgers' top minor-league affiliate for that owned in Los Angeles by the Cubs. Wrigley Field in Los Angeles, smaller than Ebbets Field back in Brooklyn with a seating capacity of only about 24,000, hardly seemed adequate for Dodgers home games in a new West Coast home. But more importantly, O'Malley had obtained territorial rights to expansion into the South California region. Then came the task of convincing Giants owner Horace Stoneham of the advantages of West Coast play as well; National League owners would look more favorably upon a plan which provided for two clubs resident in California and thus allowed West Coast road trips with two stopping points for the remainder of the senior circuit. O'Malley's true genius was to realize that air travel had changed the face of baseball and opened an immense new market on the other side of the nation, where a huge and avid population of Pacific Coast League fans were hungry for major-league status. The final piece of O'Malley's master plan was put into place in the spring of 1957 at the Dodgers' training camp in Vero Beach. Here Los Angeles city officials were convinced to launch a long-range plan which would provide rights to Chavez Ravine in exchange for the downtown Wrigley Field site which O'Malley now owned. One historian has called this last transaction the most one-sided deal since the purchase of Manhattan. Once the city fathers of San Francisco were also convinced of the financial boon involved in supporting a transfer of the ancient Dodgers-Giants rivalry to California, National League owners voted in May of 1957 to sanction such a move if only O'Malley and Stoneham would officially request it. For his part, Horace Stoneham had already realized the financial suicide which faced his own ball club if he remained behind in an aging Gotham ballpark while O'Malley and his Dodgers departed to greener pastures in the West.

One tragedy surrounding the Dodgers' move that winter, however, remained to be played out. On January 28, 1958, only weeks before the opening of spring camp in Vero Beach, Roy Campanella was badly injured in a freak automobile accident on rain-slick roads only miles from his Long Island home. Campanella was left a paraplegic and would never walk again, let alone crouch behind home plate or display his famed home run trot in the inviting confines of the Dodgers' new L.A. home. The end of Roy Campanella's brilliant yet truncated career was in so many ways ironically parallel to the demise of the Brooklyn franchise itself. The heart and soul of the "Boys of Summer" was struck down with the same unexpected suddenness that had vanquished the beloved Brooklyn franchise itself. The full measure of Campanella's loss was perhaps not realized until the 1958 Dodgers slipped into the league cellar the following spring; his unrivalled popularity was not perhaps appreciated until a May evening of 1959 when the largest crowd ever to see a professional baseball game (93,103, with a reported 15,000 turned away at the gate as well) turned out at the L.A. Coliseum for a meaningless exhibition between the Dodgers and Yankees which had been arranged to honor the wheelchair-ridden catcher and future Hall of Famer. May 7, 1959, was perhaps the most emotional night of modern Dodgers history, and a fitting tribute to a man who was as beloved as any ever to wear a Dodgers uniform. But the truest measure of Campanella's appeal among the nation's baseball fans was more likely the fact that this tribute was ironically staged in the city where he himself never played a single major-league game.

The metropolis of Los Angeles greeted the Dodgers and Mr. O'Malley with open

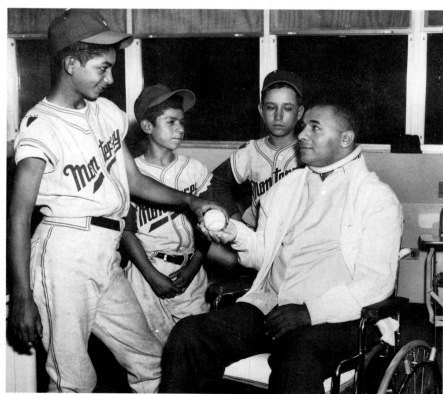

Below: *Hector Torres, pitcher for Little League Champion Monterrey, Mexico, who pitched and won the final game of the Little League World Series, hands the former Brooklyn Dodgers' star catcher Roy Campanella a baseball autographed by the entire Monterrey team, August 25, 1958. Eight months after his paralyzing automobile accident, Campy was undergoing a rehabilitation program at the NYU-Bellevue Medical Center. Campy's popularity with fans everywhere was attested by the outpouring of support which followed his unfortunate accident only months before the team's move west.*

arms during the anticipatory winter and the exciting new baseball season of 1958. After shivering through an opening series in tiny Seals Stadium in San Francisco, where the Dodgers lost their first West Coast game, 8-0, to the transplanted Giants, the new Los Angeles team arrived with the Giants for their hometown opener on April 18th, with a 2-3 record and little of the World Championship luster that had graced Brooklyn several seasons earlier. Yet the new Dodgers were greeted as returning heroes. L.A. Coliseum was overflowing with 78,000-plus fans who turned out for a slapstick 6-5 triumph against the superior San Francisco club featuring sluggers Willie Mays, Orlando Cepeda, Felipe Alou and Willie Kirkland. The opening home series drew 167,204 (55,000 per game), nearly 16 percent of the entire 1957 Ebbets Field turnout. Besides a thrill-packed major-league ball game, opening day 1958 in Los Angeles included a huge motorcade of the type usually reserved for World Series celebrations alone, an on-field, celebrity-studded, pre-game ceremony, and the largest fan turnout ever to witness a National League game. Such crowds did not cease as the summer continued, despite increasingly ragged Dodgers play, and by All-Star break the Dodgers had already exceeded the entire season 1957 Brooklyn attendance, while at that very moment they continued to languish in last place.

Baseball opened on the West Coast under bizarre playing conditions, to say the least. For starters, the cavernous Los Angeles Coliseum was perhaps the strangest and most inhospitable professional ballpark of all time. The Coliseum had been constructed for the 1932 Olympics, and had

subsequently been utilized as a college and professional football stadium. To prepare it for baseball, a steel wire fence was erected from the right-field corner across the open stretches to center field, leaving sufficient dimensions of 300 feet at the right-field foul line and 440 feet to the centerfield corner. But the close left-field stands (250 feet at the foul line) could only be shielded by a ridiculous 40-foot-high screen. "The Chinese Screen," as it was known, seemed little true protection against a potent slugger like strapping first baseman Gil Hodges, who was anticipated to pound out perhaps 60 or 70 round trippers in the ill-shaped home ballpark. The strange configuration of the Los Angeles park spurred writers and fans to comment that this was a stadium built to accommodate 90,000 fans but only two outfielders. Yet while home runs did not come as easily as anticipated (193 in 1958, which was less than in Ebbets Field in the several preceding seasons), huge paying crowds of spectators did. The Dodgers drew 1.8 million in the summer of 1958, up 800,000 over the previous year in Brooklyn. Yet the slide of Dodger veterans which had begun in 1957 continued in 1958: Snider alone hit .300; Hodges and Neal were the home run leaders with a mere 22 each; Podres led the pitching staff with only 13 victories, and Koufax (11-11) was the only Dodgers starter at .500.

The 1958 season, for all the hoopla it generated among baseball-starved West Coast fans, was clearly a rebuilding season for the Dodgers contingent that O'Malley and Alston had brought to the City of Angels. Alston's first Los Angeles team featured a tattered collage of fading Brooklyn Dodger heroes resurrected in a strange setting and presenting a mere shadow of their former

Above: *Baseball history is made as this wide angle photo records the first major league pitch in the LA Memorial Coliseum on April 18, 1958. The coliseum was jammed with an estimated 80,000 fans for the inaugural game between traditional rivals, the Dodgers and Giants. Carl Erskine is on the mound, Jim Davenport is at bat for the Giants, John Roseboro is the Los Angeles catcher, and the home plate umpire is Tony Venson. Despite the huge crowd – one of the largest in baseball history – one can note the empty seats visible in the farthest reaches of cavernous Memorial Coliseum.*

Jim Gilliam lunges at a pitch during game five of the 1965 World Series at Dodgers Stadium. This was Gilliam's sixth trip to the Series in a Dodger uniform. Earl Battey is the Minnesota catcher and Harmon Killebrew mans third base in the center background. The Dodgers would here win their third straight game, 7-0 behind Koufax, to take a 3-2 Series lead. The final outcome was a seven-game third World Series triumph for Los Angeles in just three tries, quite a reversal from the 1-8 all-time World Series ledger amassed during the Brooklyn years.

National League prominence. The 1958 and 1959 editions of the Dodgers were an unlikely mixture of veterans and youngsters as well. Snider, Gilliam, Furillo and Erskine were on their way out. Carl Erskine would win only four games in 1958 and none in 1959; Furillo appeared in as many as 100 games for the final time during the 1958 season, and Snider hit .300 and connected for over 20 homers for the last time in 1959 as well. Don Drysdale, Sandy Koufax, Frank Howard, Johnny Roseboro and Larry Sherry were the Dodgers stars of the future, and established pitcher Johnny Podres still had his best seasons before him (he would be 18-5 and lead the league in winning percentage in 1961). Yet the old order had passed and only Snider, Hodges and Junior Gilliam repeated 1955 World Series starts in 1959. The team that Rickey had originally built played under .500 ball (71-83) for the first time since before the end of World War II.

Baseball fortunes reversed themselves quite drastically on the West Coast in the summer of 1959. The Dodgers wasted no time in re-emerging as a league power on the heels of their disappointing seventh-place finish of 1958. And the rival Giants in San Francisco were not lagging far behind, completing a second consecutive strong third-place ledger and improving from 12 to only four games off the league-leading pace. The Giants actually led the close 1959 pennant race into the final two weeks of the season, but as San Francisco slipped down the stretch, the Dodgers and Braves closed fast to finish in a dead heat and create the third tie-breaking playoff in National

League history – and the third such playoff for the Dodgers franchise as well. Yet unlike the disappointments of 1946 against the Cardinals and 1951 against the Giants, the 1959 overtime series was one in which the Dodgers were not to be denied. The opening game was a squeaker, 3-2, in Milwaukee, and game two was a dramatic, double come-from-behind, 6-5 marathon in 12 innings at the Coliseum. The Dodgers' playoff victory did not come without a steep price, however, as game two was played with little rest after an all-night flight by both teams from Milwaukee to Los Angeles. The exhausting contest lasted four hours and six minutes and involved 20 Dodgers players, including six of the eleven-man pitching staff. And World Series play was scheduled to open for the exhausted National League Champions only a day later back in Chicago, against a refreshed White Sox team that had won 94 games and breezed to an easy pennant.

The 1959 World Series, like the playoffs that preceded it, was again all Dodgers, however, bringing the team its second World Championship, and the West Coast its very first. It also brought fans in unheard-of numbers to three Series games played in oversized Los Angeles Coliseum. Crowds of 92,394, 92,650 and finally 92,796 crammed the oval amphitheater for games three, four and five, each breaking the previous single-game mark of 86,288 established by Cleveland in 1948. What had taken nearly 75 years in Brooklyn was accomplished in only two short seasons in the Dodgers' new glamorous western home. Two victories and two saves by Series MVP Larry Sherry sparked a four-games-to-two triumph over Chicago's White Sox, a team with its own storied history of endless baseball poverty. Not since the infamous Black Sox season of 1919 had the Chicago American League franchise made a World Series appearance. Nor would the White Sox be destined to appear again in the Fall Classic after the 1959 season. And in the autumn of 1959 the "Go-Go-Sox" of manager Al Lopez, with their blazing speed but lackluster hitting, offered surprisingly little challenge to the hot Dodgers, who won two of three contests in both cities to claim their second world crown in club history and the first ever to be won in a West Coast city. Each Dodgers player took home a record $11,231 paycheck from the first West Coast Series, and when the final game ended with a 9-3 victory in Chicago's Comiskey Park on October 8, a jubilant Walter O'Malley threw a gala party of champagne and caviar to celebrate with Hollywood flair his team's surprise victory and his own final vindication as well.

Walter O'Malley's bold experiment had proven a smashing success by almost any standard. Crowds flocked to the ballpark in record numbers. For the first time in franchise history the 1959 Dodgers had drawn two million customers (2,071,045), becoming the fourth team in history (the New York Yankees, Cleveland Indians and Milwaukee Braves preceded them) to draw that many in a single season. The 1959 World Series had drawn 420,784, easily the largest six-game crowd in Series history. Thanks largely to O'Malley's daring plan, baseball was now a truly national sport with a genuinely national venue, with big-league play spreading from coast to coast across the nation and not just clustered within the nation's heartland and along the eastern seaboard. A new stadium to replace lopsided Los Angeles Coliseum was finally underway and promised a new age of base-ball-viewing luxury for West Coast fans. Winning baseball had also returned overnight to the Dodgers franchise, hardly skipping a beat between the final glory years of 1955-1956 in Brooklyn and the revamped Dodger lineup featuring newcomers Wally Moon, Norm Larker, John Roseboro and Maury Wills, as well as young pitchers Koufax, McDevitt, Williams and Sherry. The great Dodgers-Giants inter-borough rivalry had been preserved and even infused with a new vitality – transplanted clear across the expansive nation and drawing afresh upon the long-established baseball rivalry of Pacific Coast League cities Los Angeles and San Francisco. Only the ardent Dodgers fans of Brooklyn were left with bitter disappointment and empty memories; but for the rest of the nation's baseball fans, the national pastime had now truly entered the modern age.

Jubilant Los Angeles Dodgers swarm around relief pitcher Larry Sherry (center left and smiling) as the final out is made at Comiskey Park to end the 1959 World Series, bringing Los Angeles the title in only their second season of West Coast play. The Dodgers had just wrapped up the Series in six games with a 9-3 victory.

5. Pennants to Poverty in the Decade of Koufax and Drysdale

The 1950s were a difficult act to follow for the men wearing the blue flannels of the team still called Dodgers, despite their new home 3000 plus miles west of Flatbush and Bedford Avenue. There had been five new Dodgers pennants in a span of 20 years, topped off by two World Championships, three additional second-place finishes and a total of nine years in third place or better. The Brooklyn Dodgers of the fifties had arguably been the most talented team in a half-century of modern National League play. Of eight Dodgers in franchise history to have their uniform number subsequently retired (Reese, Snider, Gilliam, Alston, Koufax, Campanella, Robinson and Drysdale), all eight played in Ebbets Field during the 1950s, and all but Robinson and Campanella had travelled with the club to Los Angeles at decade's end. The decade began with a blaze

of dramatic action topped by the incomparable last-day heroics of 1950 and 1951 in Ebbets Field and the Polo Grounds, and it came to a resounding close with O'Malley's joyous victory party in Chicago at the conclusion of the 1959 World Series. The 1959 Dodgers had finally drawn two million fans, as their rivals in Milwaukee had done throughout much of the decade, and three 1959 World Series contests staged in the L.A. Coliseum had drawn gigantic crowds never before matched within World Series competition. Against the backdrop of such unparalleled franchise success, the 1960 Dodgers roster – crammed as it was with fading Brooklyn veterans and unproven youngsters – was hardly an optimistic sign for continued glory or for improvement.

By the outset of the 1960 season the Dodgers' lineup was dotted with new young faces and sustained with only a smattering

In classic World Series action Charlie Neal leans into a pitch thrown by White Sox hurler Bob Shaw for a long homer into the center-field bullpen during game two of the 1959 Series. This third-inning blast would give the Dodgers a lead they never relinquished in the 4-3 triumph. Neal also smacked another long solo shot in the fifth inning to pace the Los Angeles attack. White Sox catcher here is veteran receiver Sherman Lollar.

of the old guard. Heavy-hitting Charlie Neal had forced Junior Gilliam off second base by the 1958 and 1959 seasons, but Neal himself would remain a regular at that position only until the end of the 1961 campaign, when he was swooped up by the New York Mets in the league's expansion draft. Wally Moon came over from the Cardinals in 1959 and took an instant liking (despite being a left-handed batter) to the Coliseum's famed Chinese Wall in left. Moon slugged 19 homers in 1959 while leading the circuit in triples; yet his finest Dodgers summer was in 1961, when he led the team in batting at .328. Mammoth Frank Howard, an All-American basketball player out of Ohio State University, became a starting outfielder in 1960 and won National League Rookie-of-the-Year honors that season. Howard crushed 121 home runs in his five seasons as a Dodgers regular. Norm Larker (also to be lost in the 1962 expansion draft, to Houston) had replaced Furillo as the right fielder by the end of 1959, and led the Dodgers in hitting the very next season with a proud .323 average. Speedster Maury Wills broke in at shortstop in 1959 and was the regular there by the following season. Johnny Roseboro was the new catcher after Roy Campanella's tragic departure, and would catch the bulk of Dodgers games through the end of the 1967 season while both hitting with moderate power and deftly handling a wealth of promising young pitchers. Gil Hodges still anchored down first on opening day of 1960, and Snider still patrolled center, yet the former was 37 and slipped to only eight homers in 1960 and 1961 before departing to the Mets, while the latter never again hit .300 or displayed his familiar power after his last brief hurrah of 1959. Reese had retired in 1958 and Carl Furillo was unceremoniously released after feuding with management at the outset of the 1960 campaign.

While the great "Boys of Summer" teams had consistently triumphed, with awesome, long-ball power and the lofty batting averages of Furillo, Snider, Robinson and Hodges, the West Coast Dodgers of the early 1960s seemed destined to be a team meant to survive on the talents of an impressive stable of young pitching thoroughbreds. While Sandy Koufax toiled in relative obscurity his first six big-league seasons, winning in double figures only once (11) in 1958, his strikeout totals had climbed to 173 and 197 by the 1959 and 1960 seasons. Koufax also displayed flashes of true brilliance, as on the night in July of 1959 when he had established a club record by striking out 16 Phillies, and again a month later when he fanned 18 Giants to tie

Bob Feller's 1938 major-league mark. Lefty Johnny Podres had built on his sterling 1955 World Series performance to become a true mainstay of the Dodgers' staff by 1958, winning 13 games or more the first six seasons in Los Angeles. But the ace of the re-

Maury Wills, then holder of the major league record for stolen bases in a single season (104 in 1962) here demonstrates his sliding technique for the camera during training camp at Vero Beach in March 1965. Wills had already led the NL in steals for five consecutive years, and he would make it six in the 1965 championship year with 94 more successful thefts. This was also to be Wills' last season to win the crown in the base-stealing department.

vamped Dodgers' mound corps was the young Don Drysdale (22 wins in 1958), ace of the 1959 pennant-winning Dodgers with a 17-13 mark and the opening day starter for Walter Alston in all four inaugural games in the L.A. Coliseum. Another youngster, Stan Williams, became a starter in 1960 and won 14 games twice and 15 once in his three full-time seasons (1960-1962). A highlight for this young Dodgers staff came in the three-day span of June 22-24, 1960, when Drysdale, Williams and Roger Craig combined to hurl three consecutive shut-outs at the opposition.

The years 1960 and 1961 were forgettable for the Dodgers, and transition years for baseball as a whole. Branch Rickey had re-surfaced in the baseball world in 1959 with his bold plan for a third major league to accommodate America's ever-expanding love for its favorite pastime. While Rickey's dream of the Continental League died with the failure of Congress to pass legislation which would have forced big-league expan-sion, his long-range intent bore fruit when the American League announced admis-sion of two new franchises for 1961, and the National League followed suit with

creation of the New York Mets and the Houston Colt 45s by the following spring. Expansion brought an extended league schedule as well, and with the dawn of the 1960s the face of major-league baseball would change forever from the familiar eight-team leagues clustered along the nation's eastern seaboard and playing the same single-division, 154-game schedule for season after season.

The Dodgers never contended during 1960 for the pennant they had won a season earlier. Led by Dodger refugee Roberto Cle-mente, the Pittsburgh Pirates pulled stead-ily away from the Braves and Cardinals throughout the summer while the Dodgers, finishing at 10 games above .500, limped home a distant fourth, 13 games behind the pace-setters and only three ahead of the fifth-place Giants. Bright spots of the 1960 season were the emergence of Maury Wills as a dazzling base thief (he led the National League with 50 steals), the Rookie-of-the-Year honors garnered by oversized Frank Howard, and the arrival of two additional young farmhands by the identical name of Davis. Tommy Davis became the regular left fielder that summer, and Willie Davis arrived from Spokane before season's end to lay claim to the center-field position of Duke Snider as well.

Most of the furor surrounding the Dodgers' 1961 season involved Walter Alston's coaching staff, at least in the early going before the pennant race heated up. Leo Durocher had returned to the Dodgers after almost 15 seasons, this time in the capacity of Alston's third base coach, and speculation was quickly fueled that O'Malley had signed on the still colorful Durocher as an eventual replacement for Alston himself. The manager and his illustrious coach both vehemently denied any such scenario, and the issue quickly wilted when Los Angeles won 18 of their first 31 ball games and shared first place with Cincinnati by June 1st. By late June, though, the Reds — with such sluggers as Frank Robinson and Vada Pinson, and superb pitching from Joey Jay, Jim O'Toole, Bob Purkey and Jim Brosnan — had pulled ahead of the field and were able to hold off the spunky but overmatched Dodgers by four games at the wire. The Dodgers had thus managed to escape another ill-fated World Series date with one of the most explosive New York Yankees teams of all time, one featuring Roger Maris and Mickey Mantle fresh off

their incredible fence-busting performances of 61 and 54 home runs respectively. This Yankee team, which had banged out a record 240 round trippers during the campaign, again used the long ball to crush the overmatched National League entry in a short, five-game Series.

Spring of 1962 brought the long-awaited new stadium to Los Angeles and with it the final fulfillment to Walter O'Malley's bold dream for West Coast Dodgers baseball. Dodgers Stadium – dubbed Taj O'Malley by local wags and sportswriters – opened to appropriate hoopla and ceremony on April 10, 1962, before a sellout crowd of 52,564. The afternoon's only disappointment was a 6-3 loss to the visiting Cincinnati Reds on the strength of Wally Post's late-inning, three-run homer. The new ballpark itself was a state-of-the-art, multi-tiered structure arising from the dusty hills of Chavez Ravine, 10 minutes outside of downtown Los Angeles. The 300-acre plot, once littered with dry gulches and squatters' shacks, had been fully transferred to O'Malley as part of the original deal which relocated the Dodgers franchise. The city had spent several million dollars to grade and develop the site and several million more to build appropriate roads and free-

A panoramic view of America's most beautiful park, Dodgers Stadium, shot in 1971 and showing the right-field bleachers and huge scoreboard framed by the distant mountain skyline. Ballpark critic Bob Wood joins the vast majority in rating Taj O'Malley as baseball loveliest arena, and in referring to the Chavez Ravine ballpark as "Camelot" and "the major's most stunning palace," splashed in royal Dodger blue.

Sandy Koufax in action as he hurls the LA Dodgers to a shutout victory in the final game of the 1965 World Series against Minnesota. Koufax's numbers are all the more remarkable for the brevity of his 11 big-league seasons: a .655 winning percentage (165-87); a 2.76 lifetime ERA; seasons of 25-5 (1963), 26-8 (1965), and 27-9 (1966), the latter two in his final career campaigns; 2396 career strikeouts in 2324 innings, with individual season league-leading totals of 269 (1961), 306 (1963), 382 (a major-league mark set in 1965), and 317 (1966); and four no-hitters in four consecutive seasons. No other pitcher ever put up such numbers in so short a span.

ways leading to the huge concrete and steel ballpark.

The Dodgers' successful 1962 season also brought one of the most exciting pennant races in franchise history. Koufax had finally overcome the control problems that had plagued his first six seasons and had posted 18 victories in 1961; Stan Williams joined Koufax with 14 victories apiece in 1962, while Podres added 15 and Drysdale led the league with a 25-9 mark. Pitching carried the Dodgers to a lead as large as four games over the Giants in late July; Tommy Davis was batting .350 and Maury Wills was stealing bases at a pace which threatened the once-untouchable record of the immortal Ty Cobb. The Dodgers' express was nearly derailed on July 17th, however, when Sandy Koufax developed a numbness in his pitching hand, which was later diagnosed as Reynaud's Phenomenon and which had the practical result of side-lining the young lefty for almost two months of the remaining season. The Dodgers faded badly in late September and Koufax's return in the final weeks of the campaign proved ineffectual and of little help. By closing day the Giants had caught the sagging Dodgers, who still held a two-game advantage with only four to play. A final-day loss by Los Angeles to lowly St. Louis forced the fourth tie-breaking playoff in National League history, to begin at Candlestick Park the succeeding after-noon. Ironically, this was also the fourth league playoff for the Dodgers themselves, and once only (in 1959) had they been able to win such an unscheduled post-season series. Here again the Dodgers were to fal-ter under playoff pressure when a complete collapse of the L.A. bullpen in the top of the

ninth (Stan Williams walked home the winning run) of the decisive third game gave the Giants a 6-4 victory and the 1962 pennant.

What was perhaps most remarkable about the 1962 season was the degree of sta-tistical dominance in the National League by the Dodgers. Wills had indeed shattered Cobb's legendary record of 96 with 104 stolen bases. Koufax, despite his injuries, had struck out 18 in a single game for the second time, and hurled his first no-hit game. Third-year man Tommy Davis had led the entire majors in batting at .346, as well as in total hits (230) and RBIs (153). Frank Howard smacked 31 round-trippers and drove home 119 runs. Don Drysdale had enjoyed his best season ever with league-leading efforts in wins (25), strikeouts (232), and innings pitched (314). Ron Perra-noski, with 20 saves, trailed only Elroy Face of Pittsburgh in that department. Drysdale was the Cy Young Award winner and Wills had captured the MVP Award. Almost two and a half decades later, memories of the 1962 season recall an awe-some San Francisco team propelled by the bats of Mays, McCovey and Cepeda and the pitching arms of Marichal, Billy Pierce and Jack Sanford. But a closer look at the record reveals that the Dodgers in fact dominated as much or more throughout all but the final days of that memorable campaign.

And it was not long before the Dodgers were back on top as one of the most dom-inating teams in baseball. With Koufax re-turning to form and enjoying the first of his three remarkable seasons in a four-year stretch (25-5, 1.88 ERA), and Drysdale also posting another sterling year (19-17, 2.63 ERA), Los Angeles battled throughout the summer in a three-team race with St. Louis and San Francisco. A three-game sweep of the Cards in mid-September was the turning point as the Dodgers edged ahead for a final margin of six games over the Cardinals and 11 over the Giants.

For the second time in six years on the coast the Dodgers were in the World Series and the opponent was again their long-time nemesis, the Yankees of New York. These Yankees had waltzed through the American League and possessed pitching and hitting enough of their own. Whitey Ford and Jim Bouton were 20-game winners that summer and Roger Maris, Elston Howard, Joe Pepitone and Tom Tresh had all hit 20 homers or more. Yet the Yankee bats never got untracked against the strong Dodger arms, and after only four games the Dodgers enjoyed their second World Series victory over the New Yorkers in eight tries. For the third time the Dodgers were World Champions, and for the first time they had swept a World Series in the minimal four games. Koufax went the distance in the first and fourth games, posted a 1.50 ERA, and earned the first of his two Series MVP honors. In game one he struck out 15 to surpass Erskine's 1953 single-game record. The hitting stars were Tommy Davis, who batted .400, and Bill (Moose) Skowron (playing his lone season with the Dodgers), who pounded the ball at a .385 clip.

The 1963 season had been the first step in establishing Sandy Koufax as the truly dominant pitcher of his decade. Koufax had started slow, hampered by an inability to get the ball over the plate and a desire to overthrow on almost every pitch. But eventually the Brooklyn-born southpaw rewarded the patience of Alex Campanis, who had vetoed every effort to trade or option the struggling young fastballer. Once Koufax caught fire in 1961 he was the most unhittable left-hander National League batters had ever seen, and his four-year span between 1963 and 1966 is perhaps the most remarkable extended stretch any major-league hurler has ever enjoyed. With the lively left and right arms of Koufax and Drysdale, and plenty of adequate pitching help from left-hander Claude Osteen (15 wins in 1965 and 17 in 1966) and from newcomer Don Sutton (12-12 in his 1966 rookie season), 1965 and 1966 were the true glory years of the Koufax-Drysdale Dodgers. The loss of hitting star Tommy Davis to a broken ankle in May of 1965 slowed Los Angeles, and a hot pennant race involving L.A., San Francisco, Cincinnati and Milwaukee simmered into the final weeks of September. But Koufax's fourth no-hitter in as many years, this time against the Cubs in early September, along with Don

Drysdale's 20th victory in the midst of a late-season, 13-game winning streak, carried the Dodgers past San Francisco in the final weeks on route to a narrow eleventh-hour pennant victory and World Series date with Minnesota's Twins.

The Twins boasted an awesome hitting attack, paced by American League batting champion Tony Oliva and MVP Zoilo Versalles, who had led the junior circuit in triples, doubles and runs scored. Minnesota's bats looked early like they would, in fact, carry the day in the 1965 Series, but after lopsided 5-2 and 8-1 victories in Minneapolis, the Twins' bats cooled. Three Dodger shutouts over the final five games (one by Osteen and two by Koufax, the Series MVP) settled the matter in favor of the National Leaguers, and once again pitching had proven the dominant factor between well-balanced teams.

The World Series of 1966 was by contrast

Don Drysdale here matches an All-Star Game record as he delivers the opening pitch of the 1968 summer classic to California Angels shortstop Jim Fregosi in Houston's new Astrodome. It was a record five All-Star Game starts for the durable Los Angeles righty. Drysdale was also the winning pitcher of this tight 1-0 game.

Above: *Don Drysdale was to have his career cut short at the still moderate age of 33 (like Sandy Koufax before him) by a troubling shoulder injury. Neither Don Drysdale nor Koufax was destined for longevity, nor to pitch beyond the sixties decade that they so dominated. But for a brief span they formed a righty-lefty pitching tandem that was the equal of any that ever graced a big-league roster.*

Above right: *Base-stealing king Maury Wills slides safely home with a Dodgers run during the 1965 World Series against the Twins. Lou Johnson gets a bird's-eye view of the action.*

one of the most one-sided affairs ever involving a Brooklyn or Los Angeles team. The match-up between the Dodgers and Baltimore promised a Series again based upon a classical baseball confrontation of potent American League hitting and overpowering Los Angeles pitching. Youngster Jim Palmer was the leading Baltimore hurler with only 15 victories, and Baltimore had no moundsmen among the American League leaders in any statistical category. Offense was Baltimore's strong suit: Frank Robinson had just become the first American League triple crown winner in a decade, and was amply supported by Boog Powell (third in homers and RBIs and fourth in BA), as well as by the 23 homers and 100 RBIs of third baseman Brooks Robinson. But the World Series rarely follows form, and after Drysdale was knocked from the box early in the opening game – won 5-2 by Baltimore on the superb relief pitching of veteran Moe Drabowsky – the young and untouted Orioles' staff completely shut down the Dodgers' bats and ran off three consecutive shutout victories. The three complete-game shutouts were provided by Palmer, Wally Bunker and Dave McNally. While Koufax, Claude Osteen, and Drysdale pitched admirably enough in the final three contests, they were consistently overmatched by the surprising, fledgling Oriole staff which spun a string of 33 consecutive scoreless innings and compiled an unheard-of 0.50 ERA at the expense of the punchless Dodgers. The legacy of the 1966 World Series in the end was a litany of

new World Series records set by the Dodgers: most consecutive World Series shutouts suffered (3); most consecutive scoreless innings (33); fewest runs (2), fewest hits (17), fewest total bases (23), and lowest team batting average (.142).

No player has ever gone out on top quite like Koufax did in the season of 1966. He had 27 victories and only nine defeats; an incredible 1.73 ERA; 317 strikeouts in a league-leading 323 innings pitched. He was the league pace-setter in shutouts and complete games, Cy Young Award winner and second (behind Roberto Clemente) in the race for league MVP. No player in baseball history has walked away from the game at age 31 on the heels of such a season. Add to the 1966 totals the following achievements of 1965-1966: two consecutive years as major-league strikeout leader; back-to-back Cy Young Awards (three in four years); 1965 league leader in winning percentage (26-8, .765); 1965 World Series MVP; an unparalleled five consecutive seasons as National League ERA king. It is little wonder that Sandy Koufax would be elected by the Baseball Writers of America as the game's "player of the decade" at the close of the 1960s. One writer has suggested that it was as if a pole vaulter had soared above the world record and then simply failed to return to earth! But the pain in Koufax's pitching arm had become unbearable, and doctors warned that permanent disability was a probable consequence of continuing to throw a baseball at upwards of 100 miles an hour. His elbow was con-

stantly encased in ice packs throughout the latter stages of the 1966 season, and Koufax knew he was finished long before fans or teammates or front-office management dared to face that possibility. Six brilliant summers (129 victories against 47 defeats between 1961 and 1966), piled on top of six mediocre early-career seasons (but 36 wins and 40 losses), and the greatest left-hander in Dodgers history was suddenly gone.

Drysdale's greatest single achievement ironically came in the Dodgers' most disappointing 1968 campaign, his own last successful season in a 12-year span in which he garnered all but 10 of his 209 big-league victories. In June of that year Drysdale was at his flame-throwing best as he reeled off an incredible record string of 58 and two-thirds scoreless innings over a seven-game span, including a record six consecutive complete-game shutouts. One of baseball's greatest single pitching performances toppled a major-league standard that had been established by the immortal Walter Johnson, a full half-century earlier, in 1913. A little less than two months later Drysdale would top off his final blazing summer by pitching three scoreless All-Star Game innings and recording his second consecutive All-Star Game victory for the NL.

The end of the turbulent decade of the 1960s was more of a whimper than a bang for the Los Angeles National League baseball franchise. While the nation as a whole saw political assassinations, race riots in its southern cities, and violent anti-war demonstrations in the metropolitan centers of its industrial North, baseball on the West Coast was a time of disillusionment as well for the faithful patrons of Dodgers Stadium. The real unravelling had begun in January of 1967, only weeks after the Dodgers' crushing defeat in the 1966 World Series at the hands of Baltimore. Unable to stand the pain in his arthritic elbow for another season, Sandy Koufax stunned his teammates and legions of fans with an announcement of his premature retirement at age 31. The Dodgers' front office staff also faced the loss of Maury Wills. While many of the Dodgers traveled on a barnstorming tour through the Far East in the fall of 1966, team captain Wills made an unauthorized early return to the United States in mid-tour. Infuriated team officials promptly dealt Wills off to the Pittsburgh Pirates, a brief exile from which he would later return for three final, mediocre seasons in the early 1970s.

Other stars of the decade fell by the wayside as well, as Tommy Davis, slowed by a severe ankle injury, was peddled to the Mets during spring training of 1967, and veteran Junior Gilliam ended his 14-year career with retirement that same spring. The on-field results were equally depressing, as the Dodgers fell to 16 games under .500 in 1967 and 13 below for 1968. The inevitable results were an eighth-place finish – the first season at that subterranean level since back in 1905 – followed by a tie for the seventh spot a year later. Never before in National League play had a pennant winner fallen quite so low in the standings in the span of a single year.

Off-season trades during the winter of 1968 for such battle-worn veterans as shortstop Zoilo Versalles of the Twins and former sluggers Rocco Colavito and Ken Boyer from the White Sox did little to bolster the still sagging 1968 and 1969 Dodgers teams. When Drysdale was also forced into early retirement in 1969 by nagging shoulder problems, one of baseball's most potent teams of the recent modern period had been completely dismantled in the span of little more than four seasons. The fans were predictably restless as well in Los Angeles as the curtain fell on the 1960s, and the period between 1967 and 1970 witnessed the four lowest season attendance marks in the club's entire 30 seasons of West Coast play – the all-time low of 1,581,093 coming in 1968. With an aging 1968 pitching staff on which the now-departed Drysdale had been the only winner at 14-12, there seemed little reason to imagine the Dodgers could rebound from this slide at the end of the 1960s in quite the same dramatic fashion with which they had rebounded from similar slides exactly a decade earlier.

6. The Kids of Summer— Exit Walter Alston, Enter Tommy Lasorda

Below: *Bill Russell proved one of the most durable players in franchise history, surviving 18 seasons in Los Angeles (1969-86), playing in 2181 games (the most ever by a Los Angeles Dodger), and knocking out 1926 hits (third all-time in LA).*

Hurricane Larry MacPhail and the Old Mahatma, Branch Rickey, left their impact on the Dodgers organization with a seemingly endless string of matchless player personnel decisions. Walter O'Malley's legacy to Dodgers baseball and the national pastime was undisputably West Coast baseball and the Taj O'Malley. The massive stadium at Chavez Ravine remains, a quarter century later, one of baseball's most luxurious and yet fan-friendly ballparks and a mecca for West Coast baseball fans of all persuasions. But one person-

nel decision of Walter O'Malley's was also destined to shape the direction of the franchise for the coming three decades. When Walter Alston signed the first of his single-year, renewable contracts to manage the Dodgers in 1954, no one could imagine that he would still be there and thriving a quarter of a century and seven World Series appearances later.

The summer that Alston began his fifteenth year at the Dodgers' helm, 1969, had been an historic year for baseball on the whole and for the Dodgers in particular. This was baseball's centennial year, and the year when Branch Rickey's scheme for the new Continental League almost got off the ground. On the baseball map, the greatest expansion in the big-league history also came about in 1969, a fact not unrelated to Rickey's loud efforts to launch a new professional league outside of baseball's traditional establishment. Four new ball clubs were added, with Montreal and San Diego joining the fold in the senior circuit, the Kansas City Royals and Seattle Pilots in the junior circuit. Two 10-team leagues were revamped as four six-team divisions, and the annual playoff derby known as the League Championship Series was born as a boon to televised baseball if something of a boondoggle to baseball traditionalists. In Los Angeles, Walter O'Malley finally relinquished control of his team, passing the reigns of power he had held for 19 years to his competent son, Peter O'Malley. The junior O'Malley became club vice-president and chief operating officer in 1969, stepping up to president in 1970, while the senior O'Malley withdrew to the semiretirement of board chairmanship. Major-league baseball now reached all the way into Canada, yet the man who had first stretched the nation's pastime from coast to coast had silently passed from the active scene.

Peter O'Malley's rise in the Dodgers' front office was accompanied by other major changes as well, both in the club's executive suites and in the dugout simultaneously. Buzzy Bavasi, general manager since 1951, had moved on to the expansion San Diego Padres. Walter O'Malley's original master

Steve Garvey was Mr. Dodger throughout the decade of the 1970s, playing the first 14 of his 19 big-league seasons in Dodger Blue, and ranking among the Los Angeles career leaders in numerous offensive categories: third in games played (1727), third also in at-bats (6543), third in runs (852), second in hits (1968), second in home runs (211), and the all-time leader in RBIs (992). Yet the durable Garvey was perhaps best known for his clutch play, handsome Hollywood profile, and clean All-American image. Garvey also won distinction as All-Star Game MVP and NLCS MVP during his fine 1974 season.

plan for administrative transition had seemed to involve the temporary elevation of minor-league supervisor Fresco Thompson to the post of general manager while the younger O'Malley gained some administrative seasoning. But Thompson's sudden death before the 1969 season caused the father to hasten his son's ascension to power. Long-time employee Al Campanis assumed all of Bavasi's former duties. It was Campanis who had scouted and signed such stars as Koufax, Tommy Davis and Roberto Clemente, and who had remained firmly in Koufax's corner during the star pitcher's first half-dozen mediocre seasons. Amidst all the changes swirling around him, Walter Alston was still there for the fifteenth season, and his revamped team was a fixture in the first division throughout the first half of the new decade featuring divisional play. The year 1970 was, in fact, Alston's thirtieth consecutive season as manager of a professional baseball team, putting him in the longevity department

with men like Connie Mack, Wilbert Robinson and Casey Stengel. But Alston at 60 was as spry as ever as the new decade opened, and two second-place finishes in 1970 and 1971 were followed by a third-place year in 1972, and then another second place in 1973. This was, of course, within the new divisional play alignment which featured a western division consisting of Atlanta (where the Braves had relocated in 1966), Cincinnati, Houston, San Diego, Los Angeles and San Francisco.

Of the first four summers of the new decade, only the 1971 season was a truly close race for the Dodgers. In that summer they finished a tantalizingly close second to the Cincinnati Reds, losing out ultimately by only a single game. The 1971 Dodgers team featured a newly revamped roster that was the outgrowth of extensive rebuilding efforts after the dismal twin seasons of the late 1960s. Bill Russell had appeared on the scene in 1969 as a slugging young outfield prospect who had risen

rapidly through the Dodgers' lower farm system. By 1971 Russell was making his first scattered appearances at shortstop, the position he would soon man regularly until the mid-1980s. Two other promising youngsters also emerged from the minors in 1969 and enjoyed their first full flowering during the 1971 campaign. Steve Garvey played daily at third base for the first time in 1971 (he did not move regularly to first base until 1973) and Bill Buckner became an outfield regular in 1971 as well.

The Dodgers entered 1971 with a renewed spirit, youth, speed, and a new infusion of power. The most important arrivals in spring training that year were Ron Cey and Davey Lopes. Cey would become the all-time L.A. home run leader early in the next decade, and Lopes would lead the National League in stolen bases in 1975-1976 while manning second base for a full decade. Neither would make the big club until 1973, but their presence that spring was part of a bold youth movement also featuring Steve Yeager, himself a regular catcher by 1974.

Trades had also improved the Dodgers by 1971, with power-hitting catcher Duke Sims coming aboard from Cleveland, and slugger Richie Allen being acquired in a blockbuster deal with the Cardinals. This youth was balanced with a few remaining veterans from the immediate post-Koufax era. Bill Singer had moved into the regular pitching rotation in 1967 and had won 20 games in the fourth-place season of 1969. Wes Parker was a fixture at first base, where he won six consecutive Gold Glove Awards (1967-1972) and established himself as one of the game's greatest defensive first sackers ever. Maury Wills had returned from short sojourns in Pittsburgh and Montreal to reclaim the shortstop position, and was now the unchallenged patriarch of the team. Jim Brewer was still saving games (20 in 1969, 24 in 1970, 22 in 1971) as the best reliever in club history.

For the 1971 season the Dodgers had to square off with a revamped Giants team as well as with the powerful Big Red Machine of Sparky Anderson in Cincinnati. L.A. played well early and moved into second place by June, nine and a half games behind the pace-setting Giants. Still only three games out as late as September, the Dodgers had surprised the skeptics and perhaps Alston himself by staying in the thick of the race right down to the final week. The final weekend of the season brought a crucial series with Houston – the Dodgers needing a sweep to stay even with the Giants – but it was the Giants this time who held on to capture the Western Division flag.

The next serious run at the pennant came in 1974 when L.A. fielded its best team in a

Opposite top: *The Penguin, Ron Cey, is greeted by teammates Steve Garvey and Reggie Smith as he crosses the plate after homering in the first inning of game two of the 1977 World Series. Thurmon Munson is the Yankees' catcher. Cey's 228 career homers in LA is the all-time club West Coast mark.*

Opposite below: *Steve Yeager was a durable back-up catcher for the Dodgers during almost 14 seasons (1972-1985), enjoying his best summer in 1977 when he caught 123 games, batted .256, and smacked 16 homers.*

Left: *Temperamental Dick Allen was a mystery everywhere he played, and his one season in LA was no exception. In 1971 Allen posted impressive numbers for the Dodgers (.295 BA, 90 RBIs, 23 HRs), but he was traded off to Chicago's White Sox the following season for hurler Tommy John.*

Above: *The Toy Cannon unloads yet another of his best shots. Coming to the Dodgers in the off-season of 1973, Jim Wynn belted 32 homers and knocked home 108 runs in his one spectacular 1974 LA season. A drop-off to 18 homers and 58 RBI in 1975, however, soon sent Wynn packing to the Atlanta Braves.*

Above right: *Throughout the 1970s Don Sutton quietly emerged as the top pitcher in numerous all-time categories for the combined Brooklyn-Los Angeles franchise. He won more games (233), suffered more losses (181), made more starts (553), had more strikeouts (2696), and pitched more innings (3815) and more shutouts (58) than any other Dodger hurler.*

decade or more. Their 102 victories that season were the most by a Dodgers outfit since 1962, and the most for a Dodger pennant winner since the franchise-record 105 achieved way back in 1953 at Ebbets Field. The 1973 campaign had already provided indications of this renewed strength that was to come to the Dodgers by mid-decade. But 1973 will be remembered as well as one of the more disappointing in Dodgers annals. While Nolan Ryan was tearing up the American League a few miles away in Anaheim – pitching two no-hitters and outstripping the memory and standards of Koufax by striking out a big-league record 383 batters – the Dodgers were doing a September swan dive and allowing the Reds to come on strong for their second straight West Division flag.

The 1974 season was a truly historic one in sunny California, bringing with it the first all-West-Coast World Series ever played. Other events of this landmark campaign were Henry Aaron's long-awaited 715th homer (hit against the Dodgers) and, again the phenomenal pitching of the Angels' Nolan Ryan. Ryan (who would still be pitching in 1989 and recording his incredible 5000th career strikeout 15 years down the road) posted his third no-hitter and also enjoyed a 19-strikeout game.

But the Dodgers were the bulk of the West Coast baseball story that summer of Watergate and Richard Nixon. The club was strengthened by key trades that

brought relief specialist Mike Marshall from the Expos for 34-year-old Willie Davis, and slugger Jim "Toy Cannon" Wynn from Houston in exchange for veteran hurler Claude Osteen. Los Angeles started fast, losing only their first game in Atlanta on the very night when Aaron equalled Ruth's legendary record by reaching the 715 homer mark off the serving of Dodger Al Downing in Fulton County Stadium. Andy Messersmith (20-6) and Don Sutton (19-9) led the Dodgers' mound corps throughout 1974. Garvey (.312, 21 HRs) and Buckner (.314 BA) swung the big bats for most of the summer, and Jim "Toy Cannon" Wynn immediately proved his value with 32 round-trippers and 108 RBIs. Unlike their performance in 1973, the Dodgers this year didn't fold in the stretch, though they faltered a bit in mid-September when Cincinnati cut the lead to one and a half. Alston exhorted his men to remember 1973, and the Dodgers responded by hanging on for a four-game margin at the close. When individual honors were handed out that fall, Garvey capped his fine season by becoming the Dodgers' first MVP since Sandy Koufax in 1966.

The 1974 World Series was a dream come true for West Coast baseball fans. The opponent for Los Angeles that fall was the turmoil-ridden Oakland Athletics of flamboyant owner Charlie Finley. This was a team that featured such superstars as Reggie Jackson, Cy Young winner Catfish

Hunter, and Vida Blue, and supplied enough off-field fireworks to rival the 1930s Daffiness Dodgers. Charlie Finley's boys were all business in October of 1974, however, and breezed to their third consecutive World title, aided amply along the way by six crucial Dodgers errors over the short five-game series.

By 1975 the Cincinnati Reds' powerful hitting machine of Joe Morgan, Johnny Bench, Tony Perez, George Foster and Pete Rose had matured fully and left the rest of the Western Division far in the rear. The Dodgers were second in both 1975 and 1976, but fell far behind Sparky Anderson's Reds (20 games in 1975 and half that many the following season). Individual achievements were all that could be boasted in Los Angeles, but these were by no means insignificant. Steve Garvey became the first Dodger ever to collect 200 hits in three consecutive seasons, also earning three Gold Gloves at first base over the same span. Don Sutton moved into third place on the all-time Dodgers victory list by the end of 1976, and also recorded his 2000th career strike-out, again good for third place. The end of an era was also at hand as 1976 closed. The 1976 baseball season would be the last for durable Walter Alston. Fittingly, Alston achieved his 2000th career victory on July 17th. Only five other managers in the game's storied history had won that many — Connie Mack, John McGraw, Bucky Harris, Joe McCarthy, and Larry MacPhail's old nemesis, Leo Durocher.

With their many strong finishes of the decade to that point, it seemed that little room had been left for an encore, but 1977 saw Los Angeles again dominating the National League West. The Dodgers coasted that year to a 10-game final margin over Cincinnati, winning 98 games and hitting more home runs (191) than any major-league team except Boston (213) and the White Sox (192). But the big news was a new manager at the helm. With but four games remaining in 1976, Walter Alston had finally stepped down, at age 65 and after 23 seasons on the bench with his beloved Dodgers. Assistant Tommy Lasorda had been immediately named the new permanent Dodgers skipper. And for the 49-year-old Lasorda it was also the consummation of a love affair; the ex-Dodger farm hand and long-time coach had reputedly turned down at least three firm offers to manage other big-league clubs in order to wait his expected turn at the Dodgers' bench command.

The team Lasorda inherited was one well worth waiting for. Trades had again altered and improved the Dodgers' lineup — catcher Johnny Oates and been acquired from the Phillies, and talented outfielder Rick Monday had been acquired from the Cubs for Bill Buckner and reserve infielder Ivan DeJesus. Restocked with power hitting and fine defense, and paced by the 20-win season of veteran left-hander Tommy John (four other Dodger pitchers also won 12 or more), the Dodgers streaked to a first place finish and an easy playoff victory over the Philadelphia Phillies.

Autumn 1977 would witness another thrilling World Series, the sixth in 18 seasons of Los Angeles residence. But there would again be disappointment in the end, as for the third consecutive World Series match-up the Dodgers would come away without a World Championship banner to

Below: *When Tom Lasorda replaced the quiet Walter Alston at the end of the 1976 season, after Alston had remained at the Dodgers' helm for an incredible 23 seasons, few could anticipate that Lasorda was beginning an impressive tenure of his own which as yet shows few signs of coming to an end in the near future.*

Rick Monday enjoyed one of those classic baseball careers in which long seasons of solid play (241 lifetime homers over 19 big-league seasons with the Athletics, Dodgers and Cubs) were obscured by the memory of one or two glorious moments of rare achievement. First there was the dramatic game-winning ninth-inning homer on October 19, 1981, which lifted LA over Montreal in game five of the NLCS and ended the Expos' dream of becoming the first-ever Canadian World Series entry. And then there will always be the wire service photos of Rick Monday charging from his center-field post in Dodger Stadium to rescue Old Glory from a pair of would-be flag burners, right in the midst of a Dodgers-Cubs game. The date was April 25, 1976, and the patriotic Monday was playing for the Chicago Cubs at the time.

hang above Dodgers Stadium. This was to be a Series dominated by the offensive exploits of a single superstar as perhaps no single Series had ever been dominated before. It was all Reggie Jackson, as the Yankees' slugger crushed a total of five homers (with 10 RBIs), three consecutive blasts coming in the final game (on three pitches off of three different hurlers). "Mr. October" wrote his name alongside Ruth and Mantle with one of the greatest World

Series hitting exhibitions ever witnessed. In the end the New Yorkers took two of three contests in each city. For those who were still keeping track, it was the seventh Dodger loss in World Series competition with the Yankees, compiled over a stretch of nine match-ups since their first meeting in 1941.

The 1978 edition of Lasorda's Dodgers showed little sign of faltering, however. Competition in the division was more intense, as Cincinnati (92 wins) and San Francisco (89 wins) hung around until almost the final week of the season. But with a thrilling pennant race at hand between the West Division's three long-time rivals, the turnstiles clicked as never before. The Dodgers franchise set two marvelous attendance marks, being the first club ever to draw three million at their home park, and drawing a record five and a half million total spectators with road attendance added on. The Phillies again provided little NLCS opposition, and a tenth-inning single by Bill Russell in the fourth playoff game put the Dodgers in their third World Series of the decade.

The 1978 World Series would bring still another defeat at the hands of the hated Yankees. Reggie Jackson was back to inflict more damage, hitting at a .391 clip and stroking two more homers, in the first and final games. The Dodgers' bats had been the most potent in the National League throughout the 1978 campaign, as the team paced the senior circuit in slugging (.402), home runs (149), RBIs (686) and runs (727), but against the Yankees they were outhit .306 to .261 in the six-game Series, and were swept four games in a row after two opening Dodger Stadium victories. The vaunted L.A. pitching staff with its 3.12 ERA (best in the majors) also collapsed

Andy Messersmith warms in the Dodgers' bullpen. While he gained most of his baseball notoriety as a high-priced free agent signed by Ted Turner's Braves in 1976 (where he won only 16 games over two seasons) and George Steinbrenner's Yankees in 1978 (where he never won a single game), Andy Messersmith enjoyed three winning seasons for Los Angeles in the mid-1970s, highlighted by a 1974 in which he paced the NL in wins (20) and winning percentage (.769). Yet Andy Messersmith will always be recalled as the original player who broke baseball's reserve clause and opened the doors of free agency.

(5.46 Series ERA) against the active Yankee bats. Shortstop Bucky Dent (Series MVP, .417 BA) and second baseman Brian Doyle (.438 BA) were unlikely Yankee Series heroes; each stroked three hits in the 7-2 New York victory that wrapped up the Yankees' twenty-second title and eighth (in 10 tries) over the Dodgers themselves.

Optimism was buoyed, both by two straight World Series appearances and by some old, familiar faces around the Dodgers' Vero Beach camp in the spring of 1979. Sandy Koufax had returned to the fold as a pitching coach, and another trusty arm, Andy Messersmith, was also back with the Dodgers organization for a final shot at recapturing the glory that had brought him 20 victories in 1974 and 19 in 1975. The 34-year-old, free agent hurler had been released by the Yankees due to his chronic shoulder problems, and not unsurprisingly saw only sparse action (2-4, 4.94 ERA) in his final comeback attempt with the Dodgers. Some more substantial pitching help also arrived via the trade route in the form of Pittsburgh ace Jerry Reuss, as well as from the minors in the person of highly touted prospect Rick Sutcliffe. Reuss did not produce anticipated results until 1980, when he compiled an impressive 18-6 mark, but Rick Sutcliffe paid more immediate dividends. The big right-hander was 17-10, and was voted the league's Rookie of the Year in the process.

The hitting was there in 1979, as Steve Garvey remained among the league leaders in most offensive categories, and the Dodgers led the league in homers (Garvey, Lopes and Cey each had 28). But with little pitching beyond Sutcliffe (Sutton won 12 and Hooton, 11) and porous defense, L.A. was not much of a force in the Western Division during last season of the decade. The 1979 team slumped badly in the first half, falling 18 games behind the Houston Astros by early July, and then came back slowly at season's end for less-than-respectable, third-place finish and sub-.500 record. More importantly, Walter O'Malley died in late August at the age of 75, and another era had clearly ended for the storied Dodgers franchise.

If Koufax and Drysdale were the dominant Dodgers stars of the 1960s, that laurel falls upon Steve Garvey and Don Sutton in the decade of the 1970s. A cornerstone of the remarkable infield of Ron Cey, Bill Russell and Davey Lopes – the Kids of Summer – Garvey played in every Dodgers game for seven seasons, his remarkable streak ending in 1983 at 1207 games, the fourth longest in major-league history. His 211 career homers as a Dodger placed him fifth on the all-time club list, and in 1977 the 11-time league All-Star became the first National Leaguer ever to garner over four million votes in a single year's All-Star balloting. Sutton proved every bit as durable, perhaps more surprising still for a pitcher. In a Dodger career that stretched from 1966 to 1980, the handsome right-hander amassed numbers that put him atop eight different pitching categories among all-time Dodgers hurlers: wins (233), losses (181), games started (553), games appeared (558), strikeouts (2696), innings pitched (3815), hits allowed (3291) and career shutouts (52).

Right: Jerry Reuss strikes a classic pitching pose on the mound in Cincinnati's Riverfront Stadium. Reuss enjoyed five winning seasons in LA and is one of two LA pitchers to throw a no-hitter, his coming against the Giants on June 27, 1980.

Far right: Rick Sutcliffe serves up a pitch against the Cards in St Louis. NL Rookie of the Year in 1979 (17-10), Sutcliffe won only five games in LA the next two seasons and was eventually traded to Cleveland in 1981.

Davey Lopes was nearly as much of a fixture in LA baseball of the 1970s as were Garvey, Cey and Sutton. This spunky second baseman led the league in stolen bases twice (77 in 1975 and 63 in 1976), and combined with Bill Russell during these years as a solid double-play combination. Lopes even supplied some surprising power, wacking 28 homers in 1979. Lopes stands sixth on the career list among LA Dodgers in at-bats, fifth in runs scored and in triples, eighth in total bases, seventh in extra-base hits, and second behind Maury Wills in stolen bases (with 418). His career continued on with Oakland, the Cubs and Houston, eventually ending only after 16 full seasons, in 1987.

7. From Fernando to Gibson, the Tradition Continues

Dodgers historian Richard Whittingham has called Tommy Lasorda "a unique amalgam of Casey Stengel, Knute Rockne, Toots Shoor and Billy Sunday," and the unlikely composite caricature in this instance seems fittingly appropriate. Tom Lasorda is on the surface a most compelling contrast to his mentor and former boss Walter Alston. The silent and stoic Alston arrived on the scene in 1954 as a striking departure from the ebullient Durocher and the feisty Charlie Dressen who had filled the post before him. Lasorda was more in the Durocher mold, but without the mean-spirited combativeness and self-aggrandizing displays that were always Durocher's familiar calling card. Yet like Durocher, Lasorda was quite volatile, and as reported by *Sports Illustrated* columnist Larry Keith, he perhaps incited more Latin American brawls while he managed in winter league play during the 1960s than anyone since Cuban revolutionary Che Guevara! Lasorda also had Durocher's flare for Hollywood hobnobbing with glamorous stars of the entertainment and media world in tinsel town. But equally important, like Durocher again, he was also a supreme baseball strategist and skilled field general – in short, an inspiration for his troops.

It was clear when Lasorda took command of the Dodger dugout in late 1976 after five summers as key Alston coaching assistant that Tommy Lasorda's qualifications for the job consisted of far more than his welcomed and shrewd sense of baseball strategy. For Lasorda was also built somewhat in the Alston mode, despite the many stark contrasts in personality type. First and foremost the new Dodgers skipper was a fiercely loyal organization man, one who bled Dodgers blue and who always spoke as "we" and "the team," as Alston had done before him. Lasorda was also passionately loyal to his players and exerted a calming influence in the clubhouse with his youthful "Kids of Summer" teams of the late 1970s.

Much like Alston before him, Lasorda had been a journeyman player with the briefest possible big-league career. While

Right: *Manager Tom Lasorda seemingly imparts some strong advice during Spring Training sessions at the Dodgers' camp in Vero Beach.*

Far right: *Steve Garvey swings from the heels, here connecting for one of his 211 career homers in Los Angeles. Yet it is Steve Garvey's record of 1207 consecutive games played – the NL standard and third on the all-time major league list – which remains perhaps his ultimate baseball career legacy.*

Walt Alston had enjoyed but a single big-league plate appearance against the Cubs in Sportsman's Park in 1936, Lasorda pitched 13 innings with the Dodgers, and 45 with the Kansas City Athletics between 1954 and 1956, suffering four defeats and never winning a major-league contest. He had then become a career organization man whose dedication to serving the Dodgers was eventually rewarded when his own time came due. And Lasorda's reward was not without justification, for in seven seasons as a minor-league pilot in the Dodgers organization, Lasorda had won five pennants and once even been honored as minor-league Manager of the Year.

Lasorda was not the only colorful character to emerge from the Dodgers' clubhouse at the outset of the 1980s. A hefty pitcher with a herky-jerky windup and an unhittable screwball appeared from the refuge of the Mexican League, and overnight the Dodgers had their first truly colorful character since perhaps Babe Herman or Pete Reiser in the late 1940s.

Fernando Valenzuela was also every bit as much a pitching star as he was a media sensation and darling of the fans. The strike-interrupted 1981 season was the one in which Valenzuela burst on the scene with a 13-7 mark, and over the course of the summer he ruled the National League. It surprised no one who saw him pitch that year that Valenzuela was a runaway choice as Cy Young Award winner, and an equally obvious selection as the National League's Rookie of the Year. In winning the latter prize he became the tenth Dodger so honored, and the third of four in succession.

Sutcliffe had taken the honor in 1979, left-handed pitcher Steve Howe won in 1980, and infielder Steve Sax would follow suit in 1982 as well.

Valenzuela's first major-league outings actually came in late 1980, when he appeared in 10 games, tossed 18 innings, and won two decisions without allowing a single earned run. The 1980 season had seen the Dodgers return to respectability with a second-place finish, 92 victories, and a near pennant which was only lost in a one-game playoff against Houston. This was quite a rebound from the first losing season in 11 years that had unfolded only a summer earlier. The 1980 campaign saw several new young stars in addition to Valenzuela, most notably relief hurler Steve Howe. Howe carved out a Dodgers' rookie record with 17 saves (Joe Black had 15 in 1952) on his way to freshman-of-the-year honors. A milestone event as well was Jerry Reuss' no-hitter, only the second by a L.A. pitcher other than Koufax.

And 1980 also marked the end of the line for one of the greatest Dodger hurlers of all time. When Don Sutton tested the free agent market that year, signing on with Houston, he had already won 11 or more games for a remarkable 15 consecutive years while in a Los Angeles uniform, rewriting the large bulk of franchise pitching records. Don Sutton was not quite finished, of course, and he would go on pitching with Milwaukee, Oakland and California until 1987, compiling an astronomical total of 321 career wins against 250 defeats. In career wins, Sutton today ranks on the all-time list, seventh among modern pitchers.

Far left: *Reggie Smith pounded homers from both sides of the plate during five seasons with the LA Dodgers (1977-1981), connecting for 87 of his 314 career round-trippers while with Los Angeles. His career-high total of 32 came in his first Dodger season.*

Left: *Lefty Fernando Valenzuela displays his Rookie-of-the-Year form during the 1981 season, the year he also led the NL with 180 strikeouts.*

Burt Hooton here delivers one plateward. In nine seasons with the Dodgers (1976-1984), this hard-throwing right-hander won 94 games, highlighted by a 19-10 record in 1978 and an 11-6 mark during the 1981 World Championship year. Hooton was also 3-3 lifetime in his three World Series appearances, and 2-0 in NLCS play.

This was a strong Dodgers team, but not a dominant one, and only the quirk of strike-interrupted play allowed another pennant to fly in Los Angeles. Cincinnati, with the best record in baseball, did not qualify for post-season action, nipped by the Dodgers in the first half and falling one and a half games behind Houston in the second session of makeshift league play. Regular composite standings would have left the Reds three games up on the Dodgers and a full five above the Astros, but this was not to be a summer in which either logic or good form applied. Given a window of opportunity, the Dodgers seized it and squeaked by both the Astros and Expos in the bizarre set of twin, ad hoc, playoff series. The ultimate thriller came with outfielder Rick Monday's solo home run, stroked in the top of the ninth inning in playoff game five at Montreal, clinching another Dodgers pennant by a tight 2-1 score and frustrating the Expos, who had come within an eyelash of being Canada's first World Series entry ever.

Some sense of normalcy returned to baseball by October. The World Series was after all the World Series, and again it was a clash of traditional rivals. The 1981 World Series meant another shot at the omnipresent New York Yankees, and in this year of extraordinary Dodgers karma, luck would finally rest with Los Angeles and against the hated New Yorkers, for a change. National League Manager of the Year, Tom Lasorda, saved his rookie ace Valenzuela for game three on the coast, and the Dodgers posted their first Series triumph as Fernando staggered to a complete-game 5-4 victory, despite allowing nine hits and issuing seven walks. From there it was three straight wins for Lasorda's men, with Steve Howe picking up one win and one save down the stretch, and Burt Hooton hurling a complete-game five-hitter in game five. Pedro Guerrero was the batting star in the final contest, driving in five runs as the Dodgers pounded six Yankee pitchers for 13 hits and a commanding 9-2 win. Guerrero shared World Series MVP honors with Ron Cey (.350 BA) and catcher Steve Yeager (.286, 2 HRs), and the Dodgers were World Champions for the first time in the new decade and the fourth time since O'Malley had taken them west more than two decades earlier.

The strike-torn 1981 baseball season was one of the most bizarre in the century of major-league play. On June 12th the players' union walkout left ballparks emptied across the nation until August 9th, and when play did resume the owners had adopted a plan to restore the rest of the season – a plan that seemed to have been conceived by men with the baseball sensitivity of a Martian. Action would resume with all teams at 0-0; those four teams in first place on June 12th were simply declared Division winners by retroaction, and another layer of playoffs would be held before the LCS games, this time to settle the score between first-half and second-half division winners. This was a stroke of incredible good fortune for the Dodgers, who had held a mere half-game lead over the Reds when the ballparks had been shut down. It all seemed good stuff for television, but it wasn't much for the fan, who believed that the long course of the 162-game season always provided something in the way of victory by attrition, which was the very distinctiveness baseball enjoyed over all other sports.

For the Dodgers this was a year of mitigated success and tempered good fortune.

The Dodgers teams of the early 1980s were again teams in transition, and mixtures of old stars and new hopefuls. Steve Garvey moved on to San Diego for the 1983 campaign, a casualty of the free-agent market which was now dominating baseball business transactions; Ron Cey was dealt to the Chicago Cubs in January of 1983 for two unheralded minor leaguers, and Steve

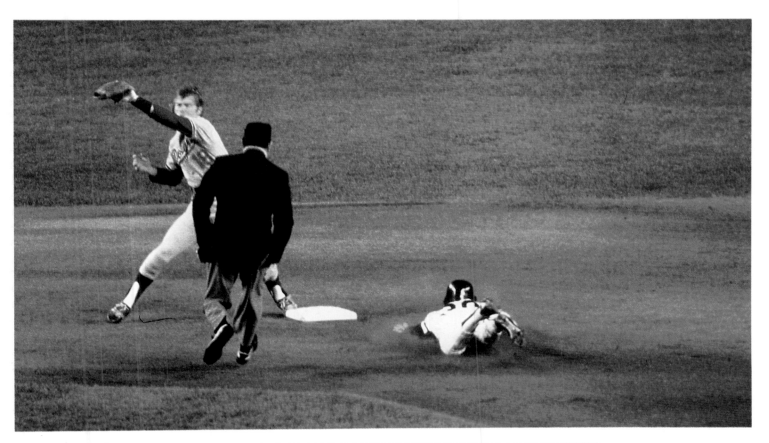

Above: *Shortstop Bill Russell fields a high throw as Yankee Willie Randolph (himself later a Dodger at decade's end) steals second during game six of the 1981 World Series.*

Left: *Jubilant Dodgers surround pitcher Steve Howe just after the final out of game six in the 1981 Series, and LA begins yet another World Series celebration. Rick Monday (left) and Manny Mota (center) are two identifiable Dodgers joining the on-field victory party.*

Right: *Dominican slugger Pedro Guerrero was the Dodgers' heavy-hitting threat of the 1980s, stroking 166 homers in 10 years for LA while also providing more than adequate play at both third base and left field posts. Guerrero hit over 30 homers on three different occasions (1982, 1983, 1985) and led the NL in slugging average during the 1985 campaign.*

Right: *Manager Tom Lasorda, catcher Jack Fimple, and second baseman Steve Sax (number 3) greet new Dodger pitcher Rick Honeycutt during the fifth inning of the 1983 NLCS game three versus the Phillies. Honeycutt would not stay around long, lasting only a third of an inning in the Dodger 7-2 loss.*

Howe lost a battle with alcohol which rendered him ineffectual long before his departure in 1985. Hurler Bob Welch, himself battling through substance abuse problems, became a mainstay of the mound corps with 115 victories between 1978 and 1987. Fernando Valenzuela proved to be no mere rookie flash, continuing to dominate NL hitters for several seasons to come, and posting 19 victories in 1982 and 21 in 1986 (his only 20-game winning season). Before being dealt to the St. Louis Cardinals in 1988, Pedro Guerrero, heavy-hitting Dominican outfielder and third baseman, became the new Dodgers' slugging star. Guerrero smashed 32 homers in 1982 and 1983, and a career-high 33 in 1985, a total of 166 over an 11-year span.

Two more division crowns would come to the Los Angeles Dodgers in the mid-1980s. After a defeat at the wire in 1982, falling by one game to Atlanta, the Dodgers hung on against the same Braves for a three-game margin in 1983. But the League Championship Series was swept in three of four by the hot Phillies of Philadelphia, paced by three homers from Gary Matthews and the stellar pitching of aging veteran Steve Carlton.

In 1985 the Dodgers won 95 and waltzed home comfortably in late September with a five-and-a-half game lead over Cincinnati. But again the playoffs were dominated by an Eastern Division rival, this time the Cardinals of St. Louis, 4-2, in the new seven-game LCS format.

The middle years of the 1980s were a time of individual achievements for the Dodgers, however. Alejandro Pena won the ERA title in 1984 (12-6, 2.48). Emerging pitching hero Orel Hershiser (19-3, .864) paced the league in winning percentage in 1985, the first Dodger to do so since Rick Rhoden (12-3, .800) had accomplished the feat in 1976. And Ron Cey finally became the all-time Dodgers home run leader in Los Angeles in 1982, stroking his 228th and also moving into fourth place (behind Snider, Hodges and Campanella) on the combined all-time Dodgers list.

The 1988 campaign was perhaps the most Cinderella-like year in all of Dodgers history, as the L.A. entry charged quickly from the gate and held on over the summer for a final seven-game margin on Cincinnati, managed by all-time career hits leader Pete Rose. A young Dodgers team was given little attention in pre-season polls, yet took the lead in the first weeks of the season and never looked back at the trailing Reds and Padres. This was an emotional team, inspired by new acquisition Kirk Gibson, who had come to Los Angeles as an expensive free agent from the Detroit Tigers. Gibson added his name to the lengthy tradition of colorful Dodgers characters early on, storming from the Dodgers' spring training camp when his teammates subjected the high-priced outfielder to some welcoming boyish clubhouse pranks. Gibson promptly returned, but not before admonishing his new mates that he had come to win and that such tomfoolery had little place in a winning organization. His emotional spring training antics established Gibson's flair for controversy, but it also inspired his Dodgers teammates. Gibson was a fitting MVP for the National League in 1988, one who demonstrated the true meaning of the award and contributed as much with his hustle and clubhouse spirit as with his impressive statistics (.290 BA, 25 HRs, 76 RBIs) and clutch hitting throughout the campaign.

The 1988 Dodgers season was also the incredible success story of pitcher Orel Hershiser, who enjoyed as honor-filled and accomplished a summer as any known by a long list of Dodgers pitching greats. The supreme highlight of Hershiser's season was his remarkable season-ending streak of 59 consecutive scoreless innings, bettering Don Drysdale's 20-year-old mark. Iron-

ically, Drysdale had recently returned to the Dodgers as a TV commentator, and was fittingly on hand to witness and describe Hershiser's prodigious feat. There was also a Cy Young Award for the Dodgers' right hander when the campaign ended, as well as league-leading totals in victories (23) and innings pitched (267).

The 1988 League Championship Series between the heavily favored Eastern Division New York Mets and the upstart Dodgers was one of the most hard-fought, surprising and bizarre in the 20-year history of LCS play. The most memorable moment was the doctored-ball incident and suspension of Dodgers hurler Jay Howell. Howell had been ejected from game two when protests from Mets skipper Davey Johnson brought an umpire inspection of Howell's glove and the discovery of illegal pine tar. The Dodgers' reliever later avowed that he had utilized the foreign substance to improve his grip on baseballs during cold weather, and that the tar had

Above: *Derrel Thomas takes a healthy cut during 1983 NLCS game action, as the Phillies' catcher Bo Diaz awaits the pitch. Thomas filled in at shortstop and several outfield positions between 1979 and 1983, enjoying his best season in his first Dodger summer, as he hit .256 and played in 141 games.*

Left: *Jay Johnstone was a journeyman outfielder who accumulated 20 big-league seasons with two stops in LA along the way (1980-81 and 1985). Johnstone will be best remembered as one of baseball's premier clowns, a leader in clubhouse pranks and off-field baseball shenanigans.*

Above: *Kirk Gibson, hero of the World Series' game one, at the plate in game four of the 1988 NLCS against the New York Mets. Injuries slowed Kirk Gibson in 1989 and he batted only .213 with nine homers and 29 RBIs.*

Right: *Eddie Murray arrived in LA for the 1989 season with over 300 lifetime homers in Baltimore and prospects as the new Dodger slugging hero for several years to come. But Murray had a rough introduction to NL pitching, batting only .248 for 1989, although he did belt 20 homers and knock in 88 runs.*

negligible impact on the flight of a thrown pitch. National League Commissioner A. Bartlett Giamatti disagreed and suspended the Dodgers ace for three games, effectively eliminating him from the remainder of the championship series. But again adversity only inspired the men of Tommy Lasorda, who responded with a thrilling seven-game triumph, highlighted by Hershiser's stellar 6-0 final-game masterpiece.

The 1988 World Series was also a time of further heroics and constant fireworks. A rematch with the slugging Oakland Athletics was a fitting venue in the second-ever all-West-Coast Series, and the men of Oakland were the heavy favorites once more, seemingly invincible behind the home run power of Mark McGwire and Jose Canseco, and the dominating pitching staff of Dave Stewart (21-12, 3.23 ERA), Dennis Eckersley (45 saves), and former Dodger Bob Welch (17-9, 3.64 ERA). The Dodgers lavished in their familiar underdogs role, however, and it proved to be Orel Hershiser and Kirk Gibson who would steal the latent thunder from Stewart, Eckersley, McGwire and Canseco. Hershiser was as dominant on the mound as he had been all season (a shutout three-hitter in game two), and Howell (with a save in crucial game four) combined with Tim Belcher, Tim Leary and Alejandro Pena to completely shut down the dormant Oakland bats in a surprisingly short five-game Series.

The most memorable single moment of this and any other Dodgers World Series may have occurred in the ninth inning of the very first game, and was witnessed by millions among the nation's expansive TV audience. If the L.A. Dodgers under Lasorda had become the team of Hollywood style and connection, then what happened that night within Dodgers Stadium was ironically fitting. Kirk Gibson, hampered with knee problems and unavailable for outfield play, strode to the plate in an uncharacteristic pinch hitting role and delivered a ninth-inning blow from which the stunned Athletics never fully recovered. The parallel with baseball fiction was so apparent that NBC rushed to the nation's TV screens the following evening side-by-side video images of Gibson's dramatic homer and the nearly identical movie episode drawn from the popular 1983 Hollywood adaptation of Bernard Malamud's baseball novel *The Natural*. Gibson made a fitting Roy Hobbs, and verified for all those doubters that baseball's actual yet mythic dimensions are equal to those of the best fiction ever produced.

Success in baseball, like anything else, is the toughest act to follow, and 1989 could never reasonably match the excitement generated in L.A. by the campaign of 1988. But the Cinderella 1988 campaign quickly turned to a pumpkin in the spring and summer of 1989. Gibson was hurt and played little after mid-season. Hershiser pitched well – perhaps better than could be hoped – but he did not dominate as in previous seasons, and with a career-high six consecutive defeats dropped to 14-14 in the seasons' final week. Veteran second baseman Steve Sax had departed to free agency and the

New York Yankees, and his free-agent replacement, Willie Randolph, did not carry an equal load. Heralded newcomer Eddie Murray, who brought 333 career homers from his 12 seasons in Baltimore, had predictable difficulty in adjusting to National League pitching. Only Jay Howell lived up to expectations of 1988, carrying a phenomenal 0.67 ERA into the final weeks of the season. The Dodgers' pitching was superb, but there was little offense with the departure of Sax and Guerrero, the injuries to Gibson, and the slumping of Eddie Murray. Also, the hot Giants ran away early from the rest of the pack while the Dodgers languished in fifth place, ahead only of the hapless Atlanta Braves. For Tommy Lasorda, now already in his thirteenth year, it was back to the drawing board in another rebuilding year in 1990 and beyond.

But at decade's close the Dodgers were still a proud franchise with proud baseball tradition on full display. Fans continued to flock into Dodgers Stadium to the tune of over three million each season. And a host of young prospects and established veterans with many good seasons left were ample indication that some of the best chapters in the history of this storied franchise were still to be written in the years somewhere just around the corner.

Above: *Orel Hershiser pitching in game three of the 1988 NLCS. World Series MVP in 1988, Hershiser emerged as the new Dodgers' pitching superstar at the end of the 1980s, enjoying a spectacular 23-8 season for the 1988 World Champion Dodgers.*

Dodger TEAM RECORDS

YEAR-BY-YEAR DODGERS STANDINGS

Year	Pos.	Record	Margin	Manager(s)
1890	1	86-43	+ 6½	William McGunnigle
1891	6	61-76	−25½	John Montgomery Ward
1892	3	95-59	− 8	John Montgomery Ward
1893	6(tie)	65-63	−20½	Dave Foutz
1894	5	70-61	−17½	Dave Foutz
1895	5(tie)	71-60	−16½	Dave Foutz
1896	9(tie)	58-73	−33	Dave Foutz
1897	6(tie)	61-71	−30	William Barnie
1898	10	54-91	−40	William Barnie / Mike Griffin / C. H. Ebbets
1899	1	88-42	+ 8	Ned Hanlon
1900	1	82-54	+ 4½	Ned Hanlon
1901	3	79-57	− 9½	Ned Hanlon
1902	2	75-63	−27½	Ned Hanlon
1903	5	70-66	−19	Ned Hanlon
1904	6	56-97	−50	Ned Hanlon
1905	8	48-104	−56½	Ned Hanlon
1906	5	66-86	−50	Patsy Donovan
1907	5	65-83	−40	Patsy Donovan
1908	7	53-101	−46	Patsy Donovan
1909	6	55-98	−55½	Harry Lumley
1910	6	64-90	−40	Bill Dahlen
1911	7	64-86	−33½	Bill Dahlen
1912	7	58-95	−46	Bill Dahlen
1913	6	65-84	−34½	Bill Dahlen
1914	5	75-79	−19½	Wilbert Robinson
1915	3	80-72	−10	Wilbert Robinson
1916	1	94-60	+2½	Wilbert Robinson
1917	7	70-81	−26½	Wilbert Robinson
1918	5	57-69	−25½	Wilbert Robinson
1919	5	69-71	−27	Wilbert Robinson
1920	1	93-61	+ 7	Wilbert Robinson
1921	5	77-75	−16½	Wilbert Robinson
1922	6	76-78	−17	Wilbert Robinson
1923	6	76-78	−19½	Wilbert Robinson
1924	2	92-62	− 1½	Wilbert Robinson
1925	6(tie)	68-85	−27	Wilbert Robinson
1926	6	71-82	−17½	Wilbert Robinson
1927	6	65-88	−28½	Wilbert Robinson
1928	6	77-76	−17½	Wilbert Robinson
1929	6	70-83	−28½	Wilbert Robinson
1930	4	86-68	− 6	Wilbert Robinson
1931	4	79-73	−21	Wilbert Robinson
1932	3	81-73	− 9	Max Carey
1933	6	65-88	−26½	Max Carey
1934	6	71-81	−23½	Casey Stengel
1935	5	70-83	−29½	Casey Stengel
1936	7	67-87	−25	Casey Stengel
1937	6	62-91	−33½	Burleigh Grimes
1938	7	69-80	−18½	Burleigh Grimes
1939	3	84-69	−12½	Leo Durocher
1940	2	88-65	−12	Leo Durocher
1941	1	100-54	+ 2½	Leo Durocher
1942	2	104-50	− 2	Leo Durocher
1943	3	81-72	−23½	Leo Durocher
1944	7	63-91	−42	Leo Durocher
1945	3	87-67	−11	Leo Durocher
1946	2*	96-60	− 2	Leo Durocher
1947	1	94-60	+ 5	Burt Shotton
1948	3	84-70	− 7½	Leo Durocher / Burt Shotton
1949	1	97-57	+ 1	Burt Shotton
1950	2	89-65	− 2	Burt Shotton
1951	2*	97-60	− 1	Charlie Dressen
1952	1	97-57	+ 4½	Charlie Dressen
1953	1	105-49	+13	Charlie Dressen
1954	2	92-62	− 5	Walter Alston
1955	1**	98-55	+13½	Walter Alston
1956	1	93-61	+ 1	Walter Alston
1957	3	84-70	−11	Walter Alston

Los Angeles Dodgers

Year	Pos.	Record	Margin	Manager(s)
1958	7	71-83	−21	Walter Alston
1959	1**	88-68	+ 2	Walter Alston
1960	4	82-72	−13	Walter Alston
1961	2	89-65	− 4	Walter Alston
1962	2*	102-63	− 1	Walter Alston
1963	1**	99-63	+ 6	Walter Alston
1964	6(tie)	80-82	−13	Walter Alston
1965	1**	97-65	+ 2	Walter Alston
1966	1	95-67	+ 1½	Walter Alston
1967	8	73-89	−28½	Walter Alston
1968	7(tie)	76-86	−21	Walter Alston
1969	4	85-77	− 8	Walter Alston
1970	2	87-74	−14½	Walter Alston
1971	2	89-73	− 1	Walter Alston
1972	3	85-70	−10½	Walter Alston
1973	2	95-65	− 3½	Walter Alston
1974	1	102-60	+ 4	Walter Alston
1975	2	88-74	−20	Walter Alston
1976	2	92-70	−10	Walter Alston
1977	1	98-64	+10	Tommy Lasorda
1978	1	95-67	+ 2½	Tommy Lasorda
1979	3	79-83	−11½	Tommy Lasorda
1980	2*	92-71	− 1	Tommy Lasorda
1981	1/4**	63-47	††	Tommy Lasorda
1982	2	88-74	− 1	Tommy Lasorda
1983	1	91-71	+ 2	Tommy Lasorda
1984	4	79-83	−13	Tommy Lasorda
1985	1	95-67	+ 5½	Tommy Lasorda
1986	5	73-89	−23	Tommy Lasorda
1987	4	73-89	−17	Tommy Lasorda
1988	1**	94-67	+ 7	Tommy Lasorda
1989	4	71-83	−14	Tommy Lasorda

* Tied for First at end of regular season, but lost in playoffs
** Won World Championship
†† Split-Season in 1981

ALL-TIME DODGERS DREAM TEAM

1B	Gil Hodges (Brooklyn 1943, 1947-1957; LA 1958-1961), 370 Career Home Runs
2B	*Billy Herman (Brooklyn 1942-1943, 1946), .304 Lifetime BA for 15 Seasons
3B	*Jackie Robinson (Brooklyn 1947-1956), First Major-League Rookie of the Year in 1947
SS	*Pee Wee Reese (Brooklyn 1940-1957; LA 1958), Dodgers Career Leader in Runs Scored
OF	Babe Herman (Brooklyn 1926-1931, 1945), .393 BA in 1930, with 130 RBI Season
OF	*Duke Snider (Brooklyn 1947-1957, LA 1958-1962), Dodgers Career Home Run Leader with 389
OF	*Zack Wheat (Brooklyn 1909-1926), Dodgers Career Leader in Six Different Hitting Categories
C	*Roy Campanella (Brooklyn 1947-1957), Three-time NL MVP
RHP	*Don Drysdale (Brooklyn 1956-1957; LA 1958-1969) Three-time League Strikeout King
RHP	*Dazzy Vance (Brooklyn 1922-1932, 1935), Three-time NL ERA Champion
LHP	*Sandy Koufax (Brooklyn 1955-1957; LA 1958-1966), Four Career No-Hitters Pitched
LHP	Nap Rucker (Brooklyn 1907-1916), 320 Innings Pitched in 1910
MGR	*Walter Alston (Brooklyn 1954-1957; LA 1958-1976), Four-time World Series Winner

(* indicates Hall of Famers)

DODGERS POST-SEASON RECORD
Playoffs

Year	Opponent	Wins-Losses
1946‡	St. Louis Cardinals	0-2
1951‡	New York Giants	1-2
1959‡	Milwaukee Braves	2-0
1962‡	New York Giants	1-2
1974	Pittsburgh Pirates	3-1
1977	Philadelphia Phillies	3-1
1978	Philadelphia Phillies	3-1
1981†	Houston Astros	3-2
1981*	Montreal Expos	3-2
1983	Philadelphia Phillies	1-3
1985	St. Louis Cardinals	2-4
1988	New York Mets	4-3

‡ Tied for First, Playoff for National League Championship
† 1981 Split Season Western Division Playoff Series
* 1981 National League Championship Series

World Series

1916	Boston Red Sox	1-4
1920	Cleveland Indians	2-5
1941	New York Yankees	1-4
1947	New York Yankees	3-4
1949	New York Yankees	1-4
1952	New York Yankees	3-4
1953	New York Yankees	2-4
1955	New York Yankees	4-3
1956	New York Yankees	3-4
1959	Chicago White Sox	4-2
1963	New York Yankees	4-0
1965	Minnesota Twins	4-3
1966	Baltimore Orioles	0-4
1974	Oakland Athletics	1-4
1977	New York Yankees	2-4
1978	New York Yankees	2-4
1981	New York Yankees	4-2
1988	Oakland Athletics	4-1

ALL-TIME DODGER CAREER BATTING LEADERS

Games Played	Zack Wheat	2318
At Bats	Zack Wheat	8859
Hits	Zack Wheat	2804
Batting Average	Willie Keeler	.360
Home Runs	Duke Snider	389
Runs Scored	Pee Wee Reese	1338
Runs Batted In	Duke Snider	1271
Extra Base Hits	Duke Snider	814
Stolen Bases	Maury Wills	490
Total Bases	Zack Wheat	4003

ALL-TIME DODGER CAREER PITCHING LEADERS

Innings Pitched	Don Sutton	3815
Wins	Don Sutton	233
Losses	Don Sutton	181
ERA (1100+ Inns)	Jeff Pfeffer	2.31
Strikeouts	Don Sutton	2696
Game Appearances	Don Sutton	550
Shutouts	Don Sutton	58
Saves	Jim Brewer	125
No-Hitters	Sandy Koufax	4

HALL OF FAMERS

Name	Position	Year Elected
Walter Alston	Manager	1983
Roy Campanella	Catcher	1969
Don Drysdale	Pitcher	1984
Burleigh Grimes	Pitcher	1964
Sandy Koufax	Pitcher	1972
Pee Wee Reese	Infielder	1984
Branch Rickey	GM	1967
Jackie Robinson	Infielder	1962
Wilbert Robinson	Manager	1945
Edwin (Duke) Snider	Outfielder	1980
Dazzy Vance	Pitcher	1955
Zack Wheat	Outfielder	1959

SINGLE-SEASON DODGER BATTING RECORDS

Batting Average	Babe Herman	.393	1930
Hits	Babe Herman	241	1930
Home Runs (Left-Handed)	Duke Snider	43	1956
Home Runs (Right-Handed)	Gil Hodges	42	1954
Runs Batted In	Tommy Davis	153	1962
Runs Scored	Babe Herman	143	1930
Singles	Willie Keeler	179	1900
	Maury Wills	179	1962
Doubles	John Frederick	52	1929
Triples	Henry Myers	22	1920
Slugging Percentage	Babe Herman	.678	1930
Bases on Balls	Eddie Stankey	148†	1945
Most Strikeouts	Bill Grabarkewitz	149	1970
Extra Base Hits	Babe Herman	94	1930
Grand Slam Home Runs	Frank Howard	2	1970
	Ron Cey	2	1977
	Steve Garvey	2	1977
	Greg Brock	2	1985
	Mike Marshall	2	1985
Total Bases	Babe Herman	416	1930

† National League Record

SINGLE-SEASON DODGERS PITCHING RECORDS

Wins (Right-Handed)	Joe McGinnity	29	1900
Wins (Left-Handed)	Sandy Koufax	27†	1966
Losses	George Bell	27	1910
ERA	Rube Marquard	1.58	1916
Winning Percentage	Phil Regan	.933	1966
Strikeouts	Sandy Koufax	382*	1965
Saves	Jim Brewer	24	1970
Innings Pitched	Oscar Jones	378	1904
Game Appearances	Mike Marshall	106*	1974
Games Started	Don Drysdale	42	1963/1965
Shutouts (Left-Handed)	Sandy Koufax	11	1963
Shutouts (Right-Handed)	Don Sutton	9	1972

* Major-League Record
† National League Record

Index

Numbers in *italics* indicate illustrations